ENGLISH GRAMMAR for Students workbook

Anne Seaton

LEARNERS PUBLISHING

© 2002 Learners Publishing Pte Ltd

First published 2002 by **Learners Publishing Pte Ltd**
222 Tagore Lane, #03-01 TG Building, Singapore 787603

Reprinted 2002 (three times), 2003 (three times), 2004 (twice), 2005 (twice)

Email: learnpub@learners.com.sg
Visit our website: http://www.learners.com.sg

ISBN 981 4070 07 6

Printed by B & Jo Enterprise Pte Ltd, Singapore

ASSOCIATE COMPANIES

R I C Learners International Limited
P.O. Box 332, Greenwood
WESTERN AUSTRALIA 6924

R I C Publications Limited (Asia)
5th floor, Gotanda Mikado Building
2-5-8 Hiratsuka, Shinagawa-ku Tokyo
JAPAN 142-0051
Tel: 03-3788-9201
Fax: 03-3788-9202
Email: elt@ricpublications.com
Website: www.ricpublications.com

Learners Educational Publishing Sdn Bhd
43A, Jalan 34/154 Taman Delima
56000 Cheras, Kuala Lumpur
MALAYSIA
Tel: 603-9100-1868
Fax: 603-9102-4730
Email: enquiry@learners.com.my

CONTENTS

PREFACE

This workbook has been written primarily for students using **English Grammar for Students** and gives them an opportunity of testing themselves on the grammatical concepts introduced and explained in that book. At the same time, the full explanations given in the introduction to each exercise mean that it may be used as an independent self-testing tool.

There are 40 units, each containing four sets of exercises, graded for difficulty from A to D. Each exercise contains 8 to 16 questions, which vary from straightforward to fairly challenging. The first answer (in some cases the first two or three) is usually provided, so that the student has clear guidance as to the kind of answer expected. All the answers are given in the **Answer Key**.

The order of the units follows roughly the order of topics in **English Grammar for Students**, but some closely related topics that are dealt with in separate chapters in that book are here brought into closer association. The intention has also been to expand and develop some of the grammatical points made in **English Grammar for Students**, so that users not only consolidate what they have learnt but also widen their knowledge.

Compiling these exercises has been an enjoyable exercise in itself, and I hope students will in turn enjoy the challenge of doing them.

I would like to thank George Davidson for timely help in the final stages of compilation.

Anne Seaton

Edinburgh 2001

1 SINGULAR AND PLURAL

Plural Forms

■ Notice some spelling rules:
- Nouns ending with **s, ss, x, z, ch, sh** add **-es**: bu**ses**, cro**sses**, bo**xes**, walt**zes**, ar**ches**, bru**shes**
- Nouns ending with **y** become **-ies**: bab**ies**, sp**ies**, stor**ies**
- Nouns ending with **ay, ey,** or **oy** just add **-s**: d**ays**, k**eys**, vall**eys**, b**oys**
- Some **-o** words add **-es**: carg**oes**, domin**oes**, ech**oes**, flaming**oes**, her**oes**, potat**oes**, tomat**oes**, tornad**oes**, volcan**oes**, zer**oes** (or zer**os**)
- Some **-f** words become **-ves**: cal**ves**, hal**ves**, hoo**ves** (or hoo**fs**), lea**ves**, loa**ves**, scar**ves** (or scar**fs**), shel**ves**, thie**ves**, wol**ves**
- Some **-fe** words become **-ves**: kni**ves**, li**ves**, wi**ves**
- Some plurals are the same as the singular: bison, carp, deer, fish (or fishes), sheep, aircraft
- Some plurals are irregular: **men**, **women**, chil**dren**, g**ee**se, l**ice**, m**ice**, ox**en**, f**eet**, t**eeth**

A Fill in the correct plural form in the following sentences:

1. Miss Lee walked in carrying a pile of _____atlases_____ . (**atlas**)

2. We have been learning about _____ in geography. (**volcano**)

3. The plate dropped and broke into two _____ . (**half**)

4. One of the _____ was injured in the race. (**jockey**)

5. _____ are places where books are kept for people to read or borrow. (**library**)

6. There are several different _____ that go to the town centre. (**bus**)

7. Put all the _____ in that drawer. (**knife**)

8. Singapore has two _____ , a daytime one and a night-time one. (**zoo**)

9. How many _____ are there when you write one million in figures? (**zero**)

10. The girls exchanged _____ and telephone numbers. (**address**)

11. Please fetch me three _____ of bread from the baker's. (**loaf**)

12. All the houses in this street have grey _____ . (**roof**)

B Fill in the correct plural form in the following sentences:

1. Did you see all those _____ flying across the sky? (**goose**)

2. You start losing your baby _____ at about the age of five. (**tooth**)

3. There are herds of _____ living around the Arctic Circle. (**reindeer**)

4. The wall is three _____ high. (**foot**)

5. The _____ and _____ were allowed to get into the boat first. (**woman, child**)

6. We found a nest of _____ living under the floorboards. (**mouse**)

7. Some animals live longer than _____ do. (**human**)

8. The military _____ make a lot of noise as they take off and land. (**aircraft**)

9. Sally laid the _____ out on the chessboard. (**chessman**)

10. The farmer owns several _____ .(**ox**)

2

■ Some nouns are always plural, for example words for things that come in twos, or have two identical sides, like **trousers**, **spectacles**, **gloves**.

■ When you want to refer to them in the singular, or put a number or quantity word before them, you have to use **a pair of** or **pairs of**:

These trousers are dirty.
This pair of trousers is dirty.

My cycling shorts are in my sports bag.
How many pairs of cycling shorts do you have?

C Put **pair of** or **pairs of** before the word in brackets, and fill the gap with the whole phrase:

1. This ____pair of trousers____ has a hole in it. (**trousers**)

2. Is there a _____ on the table? (**binoculars**)

3. That's the third _____ the puppy has chewed! (**slippers**)

4. How many _____ do you need? (**chopsticks**)

5. Here's a clean _____ for you. (**pants**).

6. Take a spare _____ . (**running shorts**)

7. There are two _____ in that drawer. (**scissors**)

8. I was being watched by many _____ . (**eyes**)

9. I've lost my best _____ . (**swimming goggles**)

10. Pack another _____ . (**pyjamas**)

11. That's a very smart _____ ! (**sunglasses**)

12. He owns at least six _____ . (**jeans**)

Collective Nouns

- Some nouns are plural and need a plural verb, although they do not end in **-s**, for example: **cattle, people, police.**

- Some group nouns for people or animals, such as **audience, choir, crowd, family, flock, gang, government, herd, team,** can be singular or plural. If you're thinking of the people or animals in the group, use a plural verb. If you're thinking of the group as a single whole, choose a singular verb.

- Group nouns for things that are **separate**, such as **a collection of coins, a fleet of ships, a row of trees, a set of dishes,** can have a plural verb. Group nouns for things that are **joined**, such as **a block of flats, a string of pearls, a bunch of grapes, a flight of stairs,** usually have a singular verb.

D Choose a singular or plural verb from the verbs in the box to fill in the gaps; in some sentences you can use either a singular or a plural verb; in some only a plural verb is correct:

is	was	does	doesn't	has	leads	needs
are	were	do	don't	have	lead	need

1. A pile of dishes _____ are _____ sitting in the sink.

2. The cattle _____ grazing in the field.

3. Where _____ your family come from?

4. Helen's string of beads _____ broken.

5. A flock of sheep _____ blocking the road ahead.

6. The audience _____ laughing at the joke.

7. A flight of steps _____ to the top of the tower.

8. The choir _____ performed very well.

9. The gang of robbers _____ all caught.

10. The government _____ keen for pupils to learn grammar.

11. The police _____ know who stole the jewels.

12. A group of children _____ walking along the pavement.

13. People _____ to relax sometimes.

14. A flock of birds _____ circling overhead.

2 COUNTABLE AND UNCOUNTABLE NOUNS

- ■ **COUNTABLE NOUNS**
  - Most nouns are **countable**. They are **separate** things or people or animals, and you can **count** them, for example: **picture**, **telephone**, **teacher**, **doctor**, **elephant**, **mouse**, **idea**, **game**.
  - You can use **a** or **an** with countable nouns: **a** picture, **an** elephant, **a** game, **an** idea.
  - You can make countable nouns plural: **telephones**, **teachers**, **ideas**, **games**, **mice**.
  - You can use numbers with countable nouns: **two** beds, **five** books, **ten** teachers, **three** suggestions.
  - You use the quantity words **many**, **more**, **few**, **fewer**, **some** with countable nouns: not **many** doctors, a **few** ideas, **some** tables, **more** parties.

- ■ **UNCOUNTABLE NOUNS**
  - Uncountable nouns are things such as **water**, **cheese**, **sugar**, **grass**, **tea**, **coffee**, **honey**, **steel**, **plastic**, **electricity**, **heat**, **music**, **advice**, **information**, **work**, **football**, **tennis**.
  - You don't use **a** or **an** with uncountable nouns.
  - You don't make uncountable nouns plural.
  - You don't use numbers with uncountable nouns.
  - You can use the quantity words **much**, **little**, **less**, **some** with uncountable nouns: not **much** water, too **little** music, **less** coffee, **some** honey.

A Write out the following sentences again with **a** or **an** in the right places:

1. We're playing game of football.

   We're playing a game of football.

2. Steel is important material.

   _____

3. Grandad's wearing hat made of straw.

   _____

4. It's difficult to ride bicycle in soft sand.

   _____

5. I'd like cup of tea without milk or sugar.

   _____

6. You can cut cheese with knife.

_____

7. Water comes out of tap.

_____

8. Apple is kind of fruit that grows on tree.

_____

9. Money is useful thing to have.

_____

10. If you want food there's soup and sandwich here.

_____

11. You need pen and paper to write letter.

_____

12. Fujiyama is high mountain with snow on it.

_____

Some, Any, A/An

- You can use **some** with uncountable nouns.

- In sentences with a negative word such as **not** or **never**, you often use **any** instead of **some**.

B **In these sentences, choose some, any, or a or an to fill in the gaps:**

1. Help yourself to ____some____ cheese and ____a____ plate.

2. Isn't there _____ ice cream left?

3. I need to buy _____ bread and _____ litre of milk.

4. Harry never does _____ work.

5. We had _____ lovely holiday with _____ beautiful weather.

6. Don't you ever eat _____ meat?

7. I've got _____ interesting news to tell you.

8. I found _____ money in _____ old purse.

9. Sam has _____ new apartment so he needs _____ furniture.

10. I want to buy _____ handphone, but I can't find _____ information about them.

11. Remember to pack _____ toothpaste and _____ soap.

12. Have _____ toast, or would you prefer _____ egg and _____ bacon?

C Choose a word from the box to fill in the gaps in the sentences below. Use each word once only:

bar	blade	~~block~~	bottle	drop
grain	loaf	lump	ʼpane	sheet
slice	stick			

1. a ___block___ of ice

2. a _____ of paper

3. a _____ of rice

4. a _____ of wine

5. a _____ of chalk

6. a _____ of blood

7. a _____ of clay

8. a _____ of meat

9. a _____ of bread

10. a _____ of glass

11. a _____ of chocolate

12. a _____ of grass

A Piece of What?

■ You often use **a piece of** before uncountable nouns. For example you refer to a chair as **a piece of furniture** and an apple as **a piece of fruit**.

D Choose a word from the box to fill in the gaps in the sentences below:

advice	clothing	~~cutlery~~
equipment	fruit	furniture
information	news	stationery
work		

1. A spoon is a piece of _____cutlery_____ .

2. A pencil is a piece of _____ .

3. An announcement is a piece of _____ .

4. A guava is a piece of _____ .

5. A chest of drawers is a piece of _____ .

6. A fact is a piece of _____ .

7. An exercise bike is a piece of _____ .

8. An assignment is a piece of _____ .

9. A suggestion is a piece of _____ .

10. A tee-shirt is a piece of _____ .

3 PROPER NOUNS

A The person who wrote the following letter didn't know where to put capitals, and has put them in all the wrong positions. Can you correct the letter?

hi , edward!

i hope You are well. we are spending easter in penang and We are having a lovely Time. on tuesday jane and i went windsurfing with dad and on wednesday We went to the Beach with mum and had a Swim in the Sea. there's Lots to do here and the Weather is very good.

we shall be back in singapore at the end of april. have you finished your Project about napoleon? miss lee wants it back at the Beginning of next Term.

jane sends her Love to You. see You soon.

peter

B Put capital letters in the right places in the names below, and add 'the' at the beginning wherever you think it is needed:

1. eiffel tower   _____

2. mount fuji   _____

3. lake superior   _____

4. leaning tower of pisa   _____

5. united kingdom   _____

6. statue of liberty   _____

7. great britain _____

8. grand canyon _____

9. black sea _____

10. new delhi _____

11. tiananmen square _____

12. brahmaputra _____

13. tower of london _____

14. merlion _____

15. indian ocean _____

16. philippines _____

17. north pole _____

18. gulf of mexico _____

19. andes _____

20. arctic circle _____

Book Titles

- The first word of a book title has a capital letter.
- All the other words in the title have capitals too.
- Conjunctions and prepositions do not have capital letters in book titles. The articles **a** and **the** do not have capitals unless they begin the title.

C **Write the following titles with capital letters in the right places:**

1. the wind in the willows _The Wind in the Willows_

2. the hunchback of notre dame _____

3. the tale of robin hood _____

4. when the machine stopped _____

5. the mouse that roared _____

6. treasure island _____

7. just william _____

8. alice through the looking glass _____

9. the babes in the wood _____

10. around the world in eighty days   _____

11. king solomon's mines   _____

12. my family and other animals   _____

13. the wizard of oz   _____

D **Here are some countries and some nationalities. Where you're given the name of a country, put the name of the people beside it. Where you're given the name of a people, put the country beside it:**

1. Filipinos   *the Philippines*

2. China   *the Chinese*

3. the United States of America   _____

4. England   _____

5. Spaniards   _____

6. Japan   _____

7. the Irish   _____

8. Great Britain   _____

9. Swedes   _____

10. Pakistan   _____

11. Chileans   _____

12. the French   _____

13. Danes   _____

14. the Swiss   _____

15. Belgium   _____

16. the Dutch   _____

17. Portugal   _____

18. Norwegians   _____

4 PRONOUNS AND DETERMINERS

Which Person?

■ Personal pronouns and verb forms are often described in grammar as, for example, **first person plural**, or **third person singular**. Below is a list to remind you which name goes with which personal pronoun.

■ Except for **you** and **it**, the pronouns have two forms, a **subject** form used as the subject of a verb, and an **object** form used as the object of a verb or preposition:

	SINGULAR	PLURAL
FIRST PERSON	I, me	we, us
SECOND PERSON	you	you
THIRD PERSON	he, him, she, her, it, and singular nouns	they, them, and plural nouns

A Say which **person** the personal pronoun in bold letters is in the sentences below.

1. Where is David? **He**'s sitting on the wall.

   (_____ third person singular _____)

2. Was the weather good? No, **it** rained all week.

   (_____)

3. Boys, don't forget to take your sandwiches with **you**.

   (_____)

4. Susan and Jane missed the bus, so **they** were late.

   (_____)

5. Hi, Sally! **You** look very smart today!

   (_____)

6. Mum says **she**'ll phone later.

   (_____)

7. Miss Lee thanked Harry for helping **her**.

   (_____)

8. Hello, Mum! **We**'re home!

(_____)

9. Come and play with Jenny and **me**.

(_____)

10. The message from George says please phone **him** this evening.

(_____)

11. Dad drove **us** to our dancing class.

(_____)

12. Pick up your jeans and fold **them** neatly.

(_____)

B **Fill in the correct personal pronoun in the following sentences:**

1. Take this note and give _____it_____ to your parents.

2. Joe said _____ couldn't come to the party.

3. Where are my glasses? Oh, here _____ are, on the table.

4. Call Anna and tell _____ dinner is ready.

5. Hello, Sam! Are _____ going to the swimming pool?

6. If there's anything missing, just add _____ to the list.

7. Helen is staying at home today because _____ has a cold.

8. Good morning, Miss Lee! May _____ carry that

bag for _____?

9. In the classroom _____ each have our own pegs to hang our bags on.

10. My twin brother and _____ are very alike; people often mix _____ up.

11. Pick up your chairs quietly and put _____ on top of your desks.

12. Harry had a sore throat, so Mum took _____ to the doctor.

Reflexive Pronouns

- The forms such as **myself**, **yourself**, **himself** are called **reflexive pronouns**.
- Here is a table to remind you of them:
  SINGULAR: **myself, yourself, himself, herself, itself**
  PLURAL: **ourselves, yourselves, themselves**
- You use reflexive pronouns:
  - where the subject and the object of the verb are the same person: I cut **myself**.
  - where the subject does something without help: Did he write the poem **himself**?
  - to emphasize a subject or object: I'll check it **myself**. I didn't watch the ceremony **itself**.

C Fill in the correct reflexive pronouns in the following sentences:

1. Did you hurt _____yourself_____ when you fell over?

2. Mum baths the baby but I bath _____ .

3. All the guests helped _____ to food and drink.

4. We are looking at _____ in the mirror.

5. Can you all look after _____ while I go out for a minute?

6. Susan is making _____ a skirt.

7. Jim, did you build that model all by _____ ?

8. A cat spends a lot of time licking _____ all over.

9. I know the door is locked because I locked it _____ .

10. The castle _____ isn't open to visitors, but the garden is.

11. Children may burn _____ if they play with matches.

12. Ben has locked _____ in his bedroom.

D Fill in the correct possessive pronouns or possessive determiners in the following sentences:

1. I've had ____my____ breakfast. Have you had ____yours____ ?

2. Jack has done _____ homework. Has Jill done _____ ?

3. This jar has lost _____ lid. Have the other jars still got _____ ?

4. Jim and Jean have made _____ beds. Has Harry made _____ ?

5. Simon, you've had _____ turn, but I haven't had _____ .

6. If you both bring _____ bikes, we'll bring _____ .

7. Ken and I are washing _____ hands. Have the girls washed _____ ?

8. We'll show you _____ photos, if you show us _____ .

9. Sally has spent all _____ pocket money, but Peter hasn't spent any of _____ .

10. Please tell me _____ names, and I'll tell you _____ .

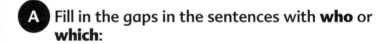

Who and Which

- You use **who** to describe a person or people, and **which** to describe a thing or an animal, or things or animals.

A Fill in the gaps in the sentences with **who** or **which**:

1. I know a man _____ keeps bees.

2. Are these the books _____ you wanted?

3. A dentist is a person _____ looks after your teeth.

4. A handphone is a telephone _____ you can carry round with you.

5. I won't have any children in my class _____ bully others.

6. Carnivores are animals _____ eat meat.

7. Did you write down the name of that lady _____ telephoned today?

8. Do you know anyone _____ could help?

9. An atlas is a book _____ contains maps.

10. Everyone _____ wanted a ticket has got one.

11. I've made a list of things _____ I need to do.

12. I've bought a CD _____ teaches me English vocabulary.

Who? What? Which?

- You use **who**, **what** and **which** to ask questions. You use **who** for people and **what** for things. But you use **which** when you mean a person, thing or animal from a **group** of two or more.

B Fill in **who**, **what** or **which** in the following sentences:

1. Lisa and Mary are twins. ___*Which*___ of them is the taller?

2. _____ is your name?

3. _____ is knocking at the door?

4. There are three schoolbags here. _____ is yours?

5. Can you tell me _____ the time is?

6. _____ wants to come for a walk with me?

7. _____ of these colours do you prefer?

8. _____ do you want to do this evening?

9. I can see two blue books. _____ do you mean?

10. _____ did that funny drawing?

11. _____ is this switch for?

12. _____ are those people in the garden?

13. _____ do you like better — swimming or cycling?

14. _____ of my friends shall I invite to my party?

C In these sentences, use **who** for the subject of the verb, and **whom** for the object of a verb or preposition:

1. From ___*whom*___ was your e-mail message?

2. The only person ___*whom*___ I recognize is Anna.

3. People _____ travel to work every day are called commuters.

4. To _____ shall I address the envelope?

5. _____ did you choose for the team?

6. _____ will make the best leader, do you think?

7. The cousins with _____ Sally stayed taught her to ride a bike.

8. By _____ was this play written?

9. I wonder _____ is telephoning me so late?

10. The man with the beard? I don't know _____ you mean.

11. All the children _____ Miss Lee teaches are doing well.

12. Tell me _____ that lady is, standing by the door.

Who and Whom

■ You can use **who** as the subject or object of a verb, but **whom** is only used as an object.

That, Whom, Which

- You can use the relative pronoun **that** instead of **who**, **whom** and **which**, but you must use **whom** or **which**, not **that**, immediately after a preposition.

D Fill in **that**, **whom** or **which** in the following sentences, using **that** wherever you can:

1. Did you find the video ___that___ you were looking for?

2. A screwdriver is a tool with ___which___ you tighten screws.

3. The person to _____ the letter is addressed doesn't live here any more.

4. Dad has an exercise bike _____ he uses every morning.

5. A bank is a place from _____ people borrow money.

6. We all like people _____ make us laugh.

7. What was the joke _____ everyone was laughing at?

8. I'm standing on the very spot from _____ the photo was taken.

9. A kiwi is one of those birds _____ cannot fly.

10. Where is the magazine _____ I was looking at?

11. Lisa is the friend _____ I like playing with most.

12. George is a boy on _____ you can always depend for help.

6 DETERMINERS: THE ARTICLES

A or An?
Short or Long 'The'?

- ■ You use **a** before a consonant or consonant sound, and **an** before a vowel or vowel sound. **A** and **an** is called the **indefinite article**.

- ■ You use **the** with short **e** before a consonant or consonant sound, and **the** with long **e** before a vowel or vowel sound. **The** is called the **definite article**.

A In Box 1, fill in **a** or **an**; in Box 2, write **the** if e is short, and **THE** if e is long:

Box 1

a or **an**

1. __a__ uniform   6. _____ hurry

2. _____ carrot   7. _____ apricot

3. _____ exercise   8. _____ umbrella

4. _____ eucalyptus tree   9. _____ circus

5. _____ hour   10. _____ handphone

Box 2

the or **THE**

11. __THE__ earth   16. _____ Europeans

12. _____ horizon   17. _____ yacht

13. _____ university   18. _____ aircraft

14. _____ end   19. _____ world

15. _____ honour   20. _____ idea

Using the Articles

■ You use **a** or **an** before singular countable nouns when you don't expect people to know which thing or person you mean.

■ You use **the** before nouns when you expect people to know which thing or person you mean, or when there is only one you could mean.

B In the following story, choose **a**, **an** or **the** to fill in the gaps.

Helen looked in __the__ cupboard in __the__ kitchen for __a__ tablecloth to put on __the__ dining table. She found _____ pretty cloth with red spots. She spread _____ cloth over _____ table, and then she went to find _____ knives and forks and spoons to lay on _____ table ready for _____ meal. 'Lay _____ extra place,' said her mother, 'because Simon has invited _____ friend.' Helen put mats round _____ table and laid each place with _____ knife, _____ fork and _____ spoon. Then she gave everyone _____ glass. 'Shall I put _____ candle in _____ middle of _____ table?' she asked. 'If you can find _____ nice one,' said her mother.

Everybody came in and sat down at _____ table. They talked about _____ things they had done during _____ day. Helen had been working on _____ project at school. Simon had had _____ piano lesson. Mum had been to _____ dentist. Dad had been at _____ office all day. Simon's friend had _____ part in _____ school play and he had been rehearsing. When they had finished _____ meal, they turned on _____ television and watched _____ news. Then they saw _____ programme about _____ disappearance of wild animals from _____ world.

C Choose adjectives from the box to fill the gaps in the following sentences. Use all the adjectives, and use each one only once:

Articles and Adjectives

■ You can put adjectives between the articles (**a**, **an** or **the**) and the noun.

busy	clean	dark	easy
enormous	~~fastest~~	grey	lucky
new	orange	orderly	smart
striped	thickest	untidy	very lazy

1. Who is the _____fastest_____ runner in this class?

2. There's an _____ hole in your sock.

3. Dad put on a _____ shirt and a _____ _____ suit to go to work.

4. He put an _____ flower in his buttonhole.

5. Mum needs a _____ _____ hat to wear for the wedding.

6. Have you a _____ pair of pants to put on?

7. That's the _____ book I've ever seen!

8. This is an _____ exercise.

9. Please form an _____ queue for lunch.

10. Our cat had a _____ escape when she ran across the _____ road.

11. Fido is a _____ dog — he sleeps all day.

12. What an _____ desk!

More Practice with A, An, Some, Any

■ You can use **some** as the plural of **a** or **an**. You can also use **some** before uncountable nouns. But in questions and in sentences with a negative word like **not** or **never** you usually use **any** instead of **some**.

D Fill in **a**, **an**, **some** or **any** in the following sentences:

1. I made myself _____ toast for breakfast.

2. Would you like _____ boiled egg?

3. _____ egg is very good for you at breakfast time.

4. There isn't _____ milk in the fridge.

5. There are _____ jars of jam on the shelf.

6. You'll find _____ little bit of butter in this dish.

7. There aren't _____ clean cups.

8. Here's _____ clean one for you.

9. Is there _____ coffee in that pot?

10. There's _____ tea in this pot.

11. I like _____ spoonful of sugar in my tea.

12. Have _____ good breakfast!

7 ADJECTIVES (1)

A In some of the examples below the adjective comes before the noun, and in other examples the adjective comes after the verb. Write each example again so that you change the position of the adjective:

1. The balloons are enormous. enormous balloons

2. a deep lake The lake is deep.

3. The grass is green. green grass

4. cold water _____

5. a blunt pencil _____

6. The nurse is kind. _____

7. black clouds _____

8. The trees are tall. _____

9. hot coffee _____

10. a thick dictionary _____

11. a powerful king _____

12. The streets are narrow. _____

13. a clever drawing _____

14. The students are hardworking. _____

15. a sweet baby _____

16. The project is interesting. _____

Forming Adjectives (1)

- You often form adjectives by adding an ending to a **noun**.
- There are many different endings that form adjectives.

B Choose an ending from the box to form adjectives from the nouns below. You will have to use some endings more than once:

-able	-al	-ful	-ic	-ish
-ive	-less	-ly	-ous	-y

1. effect   *effective*
2. leisure   *leisurely*
3. music _____
4. self _____
5. rain _____
6. danger _____
7. dust _____
8. peace _____

9. week _____
10. artist _____
11. mass _____
12. home _____
13. comfort _____
14. success _____
15. person _____
16. cost _____

Forming Adjectives (2)

- You have to change the end of some nouns before you add the adjective ending:
- final consonant doubles after one short vowel: ba**g**, ba**gg**y
- **y** changes to **i** before **-ful**, **-less**, **-ous**, but not if a vowel comes before **y**: merc**y**, merc**iful**, merc**iless**; glor**y**, glor**ious**; jo**y**, jo**yful**.
- final **e** disappears before **-al**, **-ous**, **-y**: natur**e**, natur**al**; adventur**e**, adventur**ous**, smok**e**, smok**y**

C Choose endings from the box and form adjectives from the following nouns:

-al	-ful	-less	-ous	-y

1. juice   *juicy*
2. nerve _____
3. beauty _____
4. bride _____
5. penny _____
6. study _____
7. fame _____

8. mud _____
9. play _____
10. noise _____
11. sun _____
12. globe _____
13. ease _____
14. fury _____

■ *There are various kinds of adjectives, showing, for example:*
- *size:* **large, tall, wide, small**
- *shape:* **round, flat, circular, square, pointed**
- *colour:* **blue, green, red, yellow, purple, orange**
- *quality:* **clever, difficult, happy, easy, old, new, strong, unusual**
- *origin or nationality:* **English, Indian, French, Japanese, Australian**
- *type or class:* **electric, electronic, automatic, chemical, medical, political**
- *material:* **plastic, wooden, steel, cotton**
- *your own opinion:* **nice, nasty, beautiful, horrible, lovely.**

■ *You can use two or more adjectives before a noun, but you have to put them in the right order, for example:*
- **size** *adjectives come before* **shape** *adjectives, and they both come before* **colour** *adjectives:* **a large square blue mat**.
- **size, shape, quality** *and* **colour** *adjectives come before* **type, material** *or* **origin** *adjectives:* **a long medical report; a circular plastic container; a clever paper sculpture; colourful Japanese sashes; a little red leather purse.**
- *adjectives giving your own opinion often come first:* **a splendid striped silk shirt**.

D Put the adjectives into the gaps below, in the right order:

1. a ___strange purple Indonesian___ fish (**purple, Indonesian, strange**)

2. _____ books (**academic, thick, big**)

3. a _____ tree (**narrow, dark-green, tall**)

4. _____ air hostesses (**Singaporean, charming, young**)

5. _____ clouds (**fluffy, small, white**)

6. some _____ tourists (**English, noisy**)

7. a _____ box (**cardboard, square, large**)

8. a _____ pop group
   (**crazy, American**)

9. those _____ insects
   (**stinging, red, nasty, tiny**)

10. a _____ wall (**grey,
    stone, high**)

11. a _____ magazine
    (**geographical, new, wonderful**)

12. _____ leaves (**pointed,
    yellow, long**)

8 ADJECTIVES (2)

A Choose a synonym from the box to write beside each of the words in the list below:

Synonyms

- Adjectives that have the same, or a similar, meaning are called **synonyms**.

~~difficult~~	easy	extensive	firm
handsome	intelligent	noisy	slender
soft	splendid	studious	wide

1. hard _____difficult_____

2. clever _____

3. broad _____

4. marvellous _____

5. loud _____

6. thin _____

7. quiet _____

8. steady _____

9. good-looking _____

10. large _____

11. simple _____

12. hardworking _____

B Choose an antonym from the box to write beside each of the words in the list below:

Antonyms

- Adjectives that have opposite meanings are called **antonyms**.

dull	early	~~energetic~~	gentle
graceful	hollow	light	narrow
short	slow	stingy	thin

1. lazy _____energetic_____

2. bright _____

3. rough _____

4. thick _____

5. generous_____

6. heavy _____

7. wide _____

8. fast _____

9. late _____

10. clumsy _____

11. tall _____

12. solid _____

27

■ COMPARATIVES

- You use the comparative form of adjectives to compare **two** things or people.
- You add **-er** to adjectives of one syllable:

  George is old**er** than Philip.

  George in the old**er** of the two.

  Today is warm**er** than yesterday.

- You use **more** with adjectives of two syllables or more:

  This chair is **more comfortable** than that one.

  This chair is the **more comfortable** of the two.

■ SUPERLATIVES

- You use the superlative form to compare **three** or **more** things or people.
- You add **-est** to adjectives of one syllable:

  Mary is taller than Helen and Jenny, so she is the tall**est** of the three.

  This is the thick**est** book I've ever seen.

- You use **most** with adjectives of two syllables or more:

  Who is the **most famous** pop singer in the whole world?

C Say how many syllables the adjective in the following sentences has and fill in the correct comparative or superlative form:

1. The baby is getting _____ more talkative _____

   every day. (**talkative** __3__)

2. This is the _____ hardest _____ piece of

   homework I've ever had to do. (**hard** __1__)

3. Are emeralds _____ than

   diamonds? (**precious** _____)

4. I'm glad you're _____ today

   than you were yesterday. (**cheerful** _____)

5. Who has the _____

   handwriting in the whole class? (**neat** _____)

6. Can't you think of a _____ solution than that? (**reasonable** _____)

7. Which is the _____ way to Kuala Lumpur from here? (**quick** _____)

8. This is the _____ part of the lake. (**deep** _____)

9. Singapore is a lot _____ than London. (**warm** _____)

10. I can't imagine a _____ activity than paragliding. (**thrilling** _____)

11. There will be a prize for the _____ essay. (**imaginative** _____)

12. Susan is the _____ girl I know. (**kind** _____)

Some Rules

- ■ Here are some spelling rules for forming comparatives and superlatives:
  - final **e** just adds **-r** or **-st**: large, larg**er**, larg**est**; simple, simpl**er**, simpl**est**.
  - final consonant doubles after one short vowel: bi**g**, big**ger**, big**gest**; we**t**, wet**ter**, wet**test**.
  - final **y** in two-syllable adjectives becomes **i**: busy, bus**ier**, bus**iest**; silly, sill**ier**, sill**iest**.
  - final **y** in one-syllable adjectives stays: gre**y**, gre**yer**, gre**yest**; shy, sh**yer**, sh**yest**. An exception is: dr**y**, dr**ier**, dr**iest**.
  - Besides two-syllable adjectives ending with **-y** there are a few other two-syllable adjectives that can add **-er** and **-est**: they are: clever, common, cruel (cruel**ler**, cruel**lest**), handsome, narrow, pleasant, polite, quiet, shallow, stupid.
  - Remember these irregular forms:

    good, **better**, **best**   bad, **worse**, **worst**   many, **more**, **most**
    much, **more**, **most**   little, **less**, **least**   far, **farther**, **farthest** (or **further**, **furthest**)

- ■ Note: **farther and farthest** are used for distance; **further** and **furthest** are used for distance too, but **further** also means 'more' or 'additional': **further** details.

D Fill in the correct form of the comparative or superlative in the following sentences:

1. The weather has been _____*better*_____ today than it was yesterday. (**good**)

2. Mike is the _____ boy I know. (**handsome**)

3. The journey was much _____ than we thought it would be. (**far**)

4. You're a lot _____ than you used to be. (**thin**)

5. That's the _____ joke anyone has told me for a long time! (**funny**)

6. The _____ method of all is to book tickets through the Internet. (**simple**)

7. Watching a good video is the _____ way to spend an evening. (**pleasant**)

8. Sally is the _____ of all my friends. (**nice**)

9. Is lead _____ than iron? (**heavy**)

10. That's the _____ story I've ever heard. (**sad**)

11. Where is the _____ place to cross the road? (**safe**)

12. The _____ thing to say if someone thanks you is 'You're welcome!' (**polite**)

9 VERBS: AM, IS, ARE

A Fill in **am**, **is** or **are** in the following sentences:

1. Come for a swim! The water _____ lovely and warm.

2. _____ you pleased with your new apartment?

3. I _____ very keen on keeping fit.

4. Mum and I _____ both fond of music.

5. The spectators _____ all in their seats already.

6. _____ James asleep?

7. I _____ afraid this plant _____ dead.

8. It _____ a beautiful day today.

9. Girls! You _____ late again!

10. _____ anybody there?

11. _____ Mike and Sue at home?

12. Nobody _____ willing to help.

B Rewrite the following sentences, changing full forms to short forms wherever you can:

1. Dave is in the garden. He is on the swing.

   Dave's in the garden. He's on the swing.
   _____

2. Listen! There is a strange noise.

   _____

3. Where is Sally? She is wanted on the phone.

   _____

4. Have one of these cherries — they are very sweet.

   _____

Using Am, Is, Are

■ **Am**, **is** and **are** belong to the verb **be**. You use **am** with the pronoun **I**, and you use **is** with the pronouns **he**, **she**, **it**, and with singular nouns or names. You use **are** with the pronouns **we**, **you** and **they**, and with plural nouns or names.

Short Forms

■ Here is a reminder of the common short forms with **am**, **is** and **are**:

• You can shorten: **I am** to **I'm**, **you are** to **you're**, **he is** to **he's**, **she is** to **she's**, **it is** to **it's**, **we are** to **we're**, **they are** to **they're**.

• You can also shorten **what is** to **what's**, **that is** to **that's**, **where is** to **where's**, **there is** to **there's**, **who is** to **who's**.

• You can also shorten **is** to **'s** after names and other nouns, except if they end with **s**, **ss**, **sh**, **ch**, **z** or an **s** or **z** sound. So you can say **The plate's on the table**, but you say **The vase is on the table**.

5.   What is for dinner today? I hope it is noodles.

_____

6.   You are wrong — that is a porpoise, not a dolphin.

_____

7.   I am in the car and my case is in the boot.

_____

8.   We go on breathing when we are asleep.

_____

9.   You are taller than me, but I am stronger than you.

_____

10.   Your watch is in the bathroom. It is on the basin.

_____

11.   If the car is in the garage, Dad is home.

_____

12.   There is the doorbell! The postman is early today.

_____

13.   That is Fred, but who is this?

_____

14.   You are not to telephone Granny now. It is too late.

_____

C Cross out the short form in these sentences and put in its alternative, wherever you can:

1. ~~They aren't~~ _____They're not_____ at home today.

2. ~~She's not~~ _____She isn't_____ very well.

3. It isn't _____ time to go to bed yet.

4. Robert isn't _____ fond of maths.

5. You're not _____ allowed to ride your bike on the road.

6. That isn't _____ correct.

7. We're not _____ ready yet.

8. He isn't _____ in the kitchen.

9. Susan's not _____ at school today.

10. The window isn't _____ open.

11. My book's not _____ where I left it.

12. Am I not _____ as tall as you?

There Is and There Are

■ You use **there is** and **there are** to talk about what's happening around you, and to mention other facts. You can shorten **there is** to **there's**.

■ negative short forms: **there isn't** (or **there's not**), **there aren't**

■ question forms: **is there? isn't there? are there? aren't there?**

D In the following sentences, fill in **there's** or **there are**, or **there isn't** or **there aren't**, or **is there** or **are there**.

1. _____There's_____ a clean pair of socks in the drawer.

2. _____ twelve months in the year.

3. _____ any lettuces in the fridge?

4. _____ three birds sitting on the telephone wire.

5. _____ an **e** in the middle of 'judgement'?

6. _____ no **i** in 'telephone'.

7. _____ any salt in this soup.

8. _____ enough seats for everyone?

9. How many players _____ in a cricket team?

10. _____ any spoons left.

11. _____ not enough food for everybody.

12. How much water _____ in the bucket?

13. _____ any rice in the pan?

14. You can't concentrate when _____ so much noise.

10 VERBS: THE SIMPLE PRESENT AND PRESENT CONTINUOUS

A Fill in the correct simple-present form:

1. Julia _____does_____ her hair in two long plaits. (**do**)

2. I _____ watching the fish in the tank. (**enjoy**)

3. The cat _____ indoors when it _____ . (**stay, snow**)

4. When Dad _____ work he _____ to the fitness club. (**finish, go**)

5. The soldiers _____ at least ten miles every day. (**march**)

6. Dicky _____ , _____ down on the bed, and _____ out. (**yawn, lie, stretch**)

7. If the baby _____ at night, everybody _____ up. (**cry, wake**)

8. Mike _____ everything. He even _____ to the computer. (**fix, see**)

9. Lemonade _____ , but water _____ still. (**fizz, stay**)

10. As soon as Mum _____ her office she _____ to her e-mails. (**reach, reply**)

11. Most people _____ the law and _____ to be good citizens. (**obey, try**)

12. A bee _____ as it _____ around. (**buzz, fly**)

Simple Present

■ The simple present is usually the base form of the verb:
  I **think**, you **laugh**, they **move**

■ You add **-s** for the 3rd person singular:
  he **thinks**, she **laughs**, it **moves**

■ Notice some spelling rules:
  • **y** changes to **ies**: carry, he carr**ies**
  • **ay, ey, oy, uy** add **-s**: obey, she obe**ys**
  • **s, ss, ch, sh, x, z** add **-es**: fax, he fax**es**
  • **o** adds **-es**: echo, it ech**oes**
  • **oo** adds **-s**: moo, it m**oos**

Present Continuous

- The Present Continuous is formed with **am**, **is**, **are** + the **ing** form of the verb. The **ing** form is called the Present Participle. To form it you *add* **-ing** to the base form.

- Notice some spelling rules:
  - final consonant doubles after one short vowel: ru**b**, ru**bbing**
  - final consonant doubles after a stressed syllable: refe**r**, refe**rring**
  - **l** always doubles: trave**l**, trave**lling**
  - final **e** usually disappears: bit**e**, bit**ing**; queu**e**, queu**ing**

- **ie** becomes **y**: li**e**, l**ying**

B Fill in the correct present continuous form in these sentences. Use short forms such as **I'm, we're** and **'s** wherever you can:

1. Dad *'s tying* a knot in his tie. (**tie**)

2. I _____ a letter (**write**)

3. It _____ to rain. (**begin**)

4. We _____ across the pool. (**swim**)

5. Sue and Pete _____ sausages. (**barbecue**)

6. The dog _____ the cat. (**chase**)

7. The weather _____ . (**improve**)

8. David _____ over his homework. (**puzzle**)

9. The girls _____ round the hall. (**dance**)

10. Stop it! You _____ me! (**tickle**)

11. Sally _____ to Jenny across the room. (**signal**)

12. They _____ again. (**argue**).

■ USING THE SIMPLE PRESENT

- You use the simple present to say what usually, sometimes, often, always or never happens: Mum often **works** late at the office.
- You also use the simple present for facts: The moon **goes** round the earth.
- You also use the simple present with verbs that express your thoughts, like **know, believe, think, like, love, hate, want**: I **love** music. I **believe** you.

■ USING THE PRESENT CONTINUOUS

- You use the present continuous to describe things as they happen: Harry**'s climbing** up the ladder.

C Choose either the simple present or the present continuous to fill the blanks in these sentences. Use short forms where you can:

1. The moon _____gets_____ its light from the sun. (**get**)

2. We _'re learning_ about Brazil today. (**learn**)

3. Dad _____ to his office every day. (**cycle**)

4. Humans and animals _____ oxygen. (**breathe**)

5. Miss Lee _____ a lot of facts. (**know**)

6. Look! The trees _____ about in the wind. (**blow**)

7. Blue and red _____ purple. (**make**)

8. Susan _____ an e-mail message to Sally. (**key**)

9. I _____ to be an actor. (**want**)

10. Lots of dark clouds _____ over the horizon. (**appear**)

11. The head teacher never _____ anybody's name. (**forget**)

12. The baby _____ chocolate ice cream. (**love**)

13. I _____ to do this sum. (**try**)

14. Mum _____ her hair in front of the mirror. (**do**)

15. I _____ it _____ again. (**think, rain**)

The simple present and the present continuous are both used to talk about the future.

- You can use either of them for things that have been arranged or are scheduled to happen according to a timetable, but the simple present is very common for this:

  The plane **lands** in Frankfurt at 6.30 this evening.

  We **leave** for Europe next Friday.

  or: We**'re leaving** for Frankfurt next Friday.

- You use the present continuous for things that you, or you and others, have decided or planned to do:

  Anna and I **are playing** tennis tomorrow.

  I**'m going** to the cinema with Joe on Thursday.

D **In these sentences, use the simple present for things that are on a schedule or timetable, and use the present continuous for your own and other people's plans and decisions:**

1. The train ___departs___ in half an hour. (**depart**)

2. Dave ___'s having___ dinner with us this evening. (**have**)

3. Who _____ the desserts for the party? (**make**)

4. We _____ French next year. (**start**)

5. Mum and Dad _____ to the school play tomorrow night. (**come**)

6. Jim _____ the sausages for the barbecue. (**get**)

7. The film _____ at 7.55. (**begin**)

8. The new supermarket _____ next month. (**open**)

9. I _____ Tom in town on Saturday. (**meet**)

10. Sally and I _____ the museum this afternoon. (**visit**)

11. What _____ tomorrow morning? (**happen**)

12. The new timetable _____ into operation on Monday. (**go**)

11 THE SIMPLE PAST AND PAST CONTINUOUS

The Simple Past

- You form the simple past of regular verbs by adding **-ed** to the base form.

- Notice some spelling rules:
  - final consonant doubles after one short vowel: sto**p**, stop**ped**; fi**t**, fit**ted**
  - final consonant doubles after a stressed syllable: equi**p**, equi**pped**; forma**t**, forma**tted**
  - **l** always doubles: signa**l**, signa**lled**
  - final **e** just adds **-d**: lik**e**, lik**ed**; bubbl**e**, bubbl**ed**; ti**e**, ti**ed**; fre**e**, fre**ed**
  - **y** becomes **ie**: carr**y**, carr**ied**; cr**y**, cr**ied**
  - **ay**, **ey**, **oy** just add **-ed**: st**ay**, st**ayed**; ob**ey**, ob**eyed**; enj**oy**, enj**oyed**.

Three exceptions are: la**y**, l**aid**; pa**y**, p**aid**; sa**y**, s**aid**

- But there are many irregular verbs that don't follow these rules. You will find them in the table of irregular verbs at the end of **English Grammar for Students**.

- You use the simple past to talk about happenings in the past and in stories.

A Fill in the correct simple past form in these sentences:

1. The Prince _____changed_____ into a frog. (**change**)

2. The dog _____ the sausages in the butcher's window. (**eye**)

3. Dan _____ to mend the broken jug. (**try**)

4. Sorry! I _____ . the wrong number. (**dial**)

5. He _____ his money in two years. (**double**)

6. The King _____ all the prisoners. (**pardon**).

7. I _____ the dog's head. (**pat**)

8. We _____ from one city to the next. (**journey**).

9. Last term Ben _____ the desk nearest the window. (**occupy**)

10. Mum _____ out of the nursery. (**tiptoe**).

11. Dad _____ the waiter for the meal. (**pay**)

12. I _____ home after school. (**hurry**)

B Fill in **was** or **were** in the following sentences. Where there's a **not** in the sentence, cross it out and use the shortened form **wasn't** or **weren't**.

1. I ___wasn't___ ~~not~~ able to go to school yesterday because I ___was___ ill.

2. There _____ not enough chairs for all the people who _____ at the meeting.

3. Dad _____ at home when I returned from school, but Mum _____ not.

4. _____ you very upset when you _____ not chosen for the team?

5. Dave _____ keen to go fishing but Harry and Joe _____ not.

6. Yesterday _____ not a fine day, but Monday and Tuesday _____ .

7. It _____ not as cold and wet yesterday as it _____ the day before.

8. The students _____ all very happy when their exams _____ over.

9. Anna and I _____ very early, and Harry _____ very late.

10. Children! You _____ not at your desks when I _____ ready to begin.

11. There _____ not a single person on the beach when I _____ there.

12. Dad _____ not in the house and he _____ not in the garden either.

Was and Were

- You use **was** and **were** as the simple past of **be**.

- You use **was** with the pronouns **I**, **he**, **she**, **it**, and with singular nouns or names.

- You use **were** with the pronouns **you**, **we**, **they** and with plural nouns or names.

- You can shorten **was not** to **wasn't** and **were not** to **weren't**.

C Fill in the correct form of the past continuous in the following sentences. Where there's a **not**, cross it out and use the short form **wasn't** or **weren't**.

1. Jack _____was talking_____ to Joe in the gymnasium. (**talk**)

2. The children _____weren't_____ ~~not~~ _____finding_____ the work very easy. (**find**)

3. Why _____were_____ you _____nodding_____ just then? (**nod**)

4. _____Was_____ it _____raining_____ last night?

5. The traffic _____ along the road. (**thunder**)

6. Miss Lee _____ something on the chalkboard. (**write**)

7. I'm sure Susan _____ not _____ . (**lie**).

8. Dad and Mum _____ to a concert. (**listen**)

9. _____ you _____ to get me on my handphone just now? (**try**)

10. Someone _____ at the window. (**tap**)

11. Try harder, children! You _____ not _____ loud enough. (**sing**)

12. What _____ Harry _____ on the phone? (**say**)

13. The men _____ a large box into the hall. (**carry**)

14. A lot of people _____ outside the cinema. (**queue**)

15. _____ anybody _____ in the classroom? (**sit**)

16. Why _____ the bell _____ ? (**ring**)

41

Simple Past and Past Continuous

WHAT WERE YOU DOING WHEN … ?

■ You often use the past continuous to say what **was going on** (past continuous) when something **happened** (simple past).

D Fill in the past continuous and the simple past in each of the following sentences.

1. I ___was washing___ the dishes when the doorbell ___rang___ . (**wash, ring**)

2. What ___was___ he ___doing___ when you ___saw___ him? (**do, see**)

3. George _____ out of the window when he _____ something odd. (**stare, notice**)

4. Dad _____ still _____ when the plane _____ . (**sleep, land**)

5. We _____ through the woods when we _____ a ring on the ground. (**wander, spot**)

6. The pupils _____ all _____ round the classroom when in _____ the head teacher. (**run, walk**)

7. Where _____ you _____ when we _____ you? (**go, meet**)

8. When Susan _____ to fetch me, I _____ still _____ dressed. (**come, get**)

9. My family and I _____ television when we _____ a loud bang. (**watch, hear**)

10. Mum _____ the grass when the hurricane _____ . (**cut, begin**)

11. When Miss Lee _____ 'Stop writing!' I _____ just _____ the last question. (**call, finish**)

12. I _____ of nothing in particular when an idea _____ me. (**think, strike**)

12 THE VERB *HAVE*

A Fill in the correct form of **have** in the following sentences:

1. I _____have_____ a shower in the morning, but my brother _____has_____ one in the evening.

2. We're _____having_____ a football practice this evening.

3. Dan _____ two sisters and I _____ one brother.

4. I _____ a great party for my birthday last week.

5. Our cat's _____ kittens very soon.

6. We usually _____ dinner at 7 o'clock.

7. Mum's _____ a rest on the sofa.

8. My brother _____ two tries at his driving test before he passed it.

9. This teapot _____ a hole in it.

10. We _____ to do an hour's homework every day.

11. Aren't you _____ any breakfast today?

12. Miss Lee _____ a bad cold last week.

13. Our apartment _____ two bathrooms.

14. Mum often _____ to work late at her office.

15. Most people in my class _____ dark eyes.

16. I'm _____ my hair cut tomorrow.

Have as an Ordinary Verb

- You use **have** with **I**, **you**, **we**, **they** and plural nouns.
- You use **has** with **he**, **she**, **it** and singular nouns.
- The simple past is **had**.

■ You form the present perfect of any verb with **have** + the past participle of the verb: I **have telephoned** everybody.

■ For most verbs the past participle is the same as the simple past. But there are lots of irregular past participles. Find them in the table of irregular verbs in **English Grammar for Students**.

■ You use the present perfect tense when you talk about happenings in the past that affect or explain the present: I **have lost** my purse, so I have no money.

■ You can use the shortened forms **I've**, **you've**, **we've**, **they've**, **he's**, **she's**, **it's**. You can also shorten **there has**, **who has** and **what has** to **there's**, **who's** and **what's**, and use **'s** instead of **has** after names and other nouns: John**'s arrived**. My book**'s disappeared**.

■ You can shorten **have not** to **haven't** and **has not** to **hasn't**.

B Fill in the present perfect in the following sentences, using shortened forms wherever you can:

1. We _____'ve_____ nearly __finished__ the project. (**finish**)

2. I __haven't__ ~~not~~ __made__ my bed yet. (**make**)

3. I_____ already _____ this movie. (**see**)

4. You _____ my name wrong. (**spell**)

5. _____ you _____ your purse yet? (**find**)

6. There _____ another earthquake in Peru. (**be**)

7. Sam and Harry _____ not _____ the sausages yet. (**buy**)

8. What _____ to my hat? (**happen**)

9. _____ somebody _____ on it? (**sit**)

10. It _____ raining at last. (**stop**)

11. Philip _____ the drawing competition. (**win**)

12. Who _____ already _____ Britain? (**visit**)

13. Where _____ they _____ their car? (**park**)

14. The programme _____ not _____ yet. (**begin**)

15. The sun _____ behind a cloud. (**go**)

16. I hope you _____ not _____ the packet away. (**throw**)

C Some of the following sentences use **have** and some use **have got**. Can you write the sentences again, changing the **have** forms to **have got** forms, and the **have got** forms to **have** forms?

1. Sheila's got long hair.

   Sheila has long hair.

2. We have a little black kitten.

   We've got a little black kitten.

3. Joe has to finish his maths.

   _____

4. Have you a computer of your own?

   _____

5. They've got some new videos in the shop.

   _____

6. I haven't enough money for the bus.

   _____

7. Who's got my handphone?

   _____

8. Miss Lee has an apartment near the school.

   _____

9. Has Jane any brothers or sisters?

   _____

10. Bob has only one sister.

_____

11. Pigs have curly tails.

_____

12. We've got to go now.

_____

Simple Past and Present Perfect

■ You use the present perfect with **just** and **already**: I**'ve** just **read** your e-mail message.

■ You use the simple past in stories, and with past-time words such was **yesterday**, **last year**, **a long time ago**: Your parcel **arrived** a week ago.

D Complete the following sentences using the time expression, and either the present perfect or the simple past of the verb; use shortened forms wherever you can:

1. The workmen ___have already left___ . (already, leave)

2. The rain ___began an hour ago___ . (begin, an hour ago)

3. Our team _____ . (lose, yesterday)

4. Susie's cat _____ . (disappear, last night)

5. They _____ what to do. (already, decide)

6. The plane _____ . (land, five minutes ago)

7. The programme _____ . (just, finish)

8. My computer _____ . (crash, this morning)

9. The twelve princesses _____ . (dance, till dawn)

10. The kettle _____ . (just, boil)

11. Two prisoners _____ . (escape, last night)

12. All the bells _____ . (ring, on Christmas Day)

13 Do

A Fill in the correct part of **do** in the following sentences:

1. Mum's ___doing___ her hair in front of the mirror.

2. Have you ___done___ your English homework yet?

3. Dad _____ his exercises in the morning but I _____ mine at night.

4. Yesterday I _____ 30 press-ups in the gym.

5. I was still _____ my maths when you called.

6. We sometimes _____ our schoolwork out of doors.

7. You all _____ well in last week's spelling test.

8. I _____ my piano practice before I leave for school.

9. Mum usually _____ all the shopping at the supermarket.

10. Yesterday's storm _____ a lot of damage to the trees.

Do as an Ordinary Verb

■ You use **do** with **I, you, we, they**, and with plural nouns.

■ You use **does** with **he, she, it** and with singular nouns.

■ The simple past of **do** is **did**, and the past participle is **done**.

B Fill in the negative verbs in the following sentences, using shortened forms:

1. I ___didn't go___ swimming yesterday. (**go**)

2. I ___don't want___ anything more to eat. (**want**)

3. We _____ usually _____ a big lunch. (**eat**)

4. Our baby _____ carrots. (**like**)

5. I _____ hard enough for my exams last term. (**work**)

Do as a Helping Verb: forming Negatives

■ You form the negatives of most verbs with **do, does** or **did** + **not** + base form of the verb.

■ You can shorten **do not** to **don't**, **does not** to **doesn't** and **did not** to **didn't**.

6. Dad _____ it's going to rain. (**think**)

7. My big brother _____ often _____ with me. (**play**)

8. It _____ in our part of the world. (**snow**).

9. They _____ always _____ abroad for their holidays. (**travel**)

10. We _____ any fish yesterday. (**catch**)

11. The senior pupils _____ school till 4 o'clock most days. (**leave**)

12. I _____ at all last night. (**sleep**)

13. Miss Lee _____ us a spelling test every week. (**give**)

14. Mum _____ usually _____ home till 6 o'clock. (**get**)

Do as a Helping Verb: forming Questions

■ To form questions with most verbs, you use **do**, **does** or **did** + base form of the verb.

■ In questions, the helping verb comes before the subject of the sentence: **Does** it always **rain** in Britain? Where **did** you **go** for your holidays?

C **Fill in the question form of the verbs in the following questions:**

1. _____Does_____ the supermarket _____stay_____ open till 10 o'clock this evening? (**stay**)

2. _____Do_____ I _____look_____ fat in these shorts? (**look**)

3. Where _____ you _____ to eat tonight? (**want**)

4. _____ you _____ the painting exhibition last week? (**visit**)

5. _____ the twins _____ the same subjects? (**like**)

6. What _____ a mynah bird _____ like when it talks? (**sound**)

7. _____ these trees _____ flowers? (**produce**)

8. _____ your mum _____ gardening? (**enjoy**)

9. To whom _____ you _____ that letter yesterday? (**address**)

10. Why _____ Miss Lee _____ this sum wrong? (**mark**)

11. _____ the bus _____ here regularly? (**stop**)

12. _____ you _____ any of the people here? (**know**)

13. How _____ you _____ in yesterday's test? (**do**)

14. _____ all tarantulas _____ furry legs? (**have**)

D Some of the sentences below use the **have got** form and some use the **do have** form. Can you write the sentences again, changing the **do have** forms to **have got** forms, and the **have got** forms to **do have** forms?

1. Do you have a match?

   Have you got a match?

2. I don't have time to read comics.

   I haven't got time to read comics.

3. Does the ball have to land in this square?

   _____

4. Have you got any brothers or sisters?

   _____

5. Does your mum have a map of the town?

   _____

6. Manx cats don't have tails.

   _____

Have Got and Do Have

■ When you're talking about possession, you can say, for example:

I **haven't** a pen

I **haven't got** a pen

I **don't have** a pen.

■ In questions, you can ask, for example:

Have you a pen?

Have you **got** a pen?

Do you **have** a pen?

■ When you're talking about necessity, you can say, for example:

Have you **got to** hurry?

Do you **have to** hurry?

I **haven't got to** hurry.

I **don't have to** hurry.

7. I haven't got to leave yet.

   _____

8. Do we have to bring our own sandwiches?

   _____

9. What have you got in that box?

   _____

10. I don't have the slightest idea what you mean.

    _____

11. Do they have enough food for all of us?

    _____

12. You don't have to shout like that.

    _____

14 SHORT ANSWERS AND QUESTION TAGS: BE, HAVE, DO

A Complete the short answers in the following exercise.

1. Do you think it's going to rain? Yes, _____I do_____ .

2. Has Joe finished his homework? No, _____he hasn't_____ .

3. Is the tea still hot? Yes, _____ .

4. Does Philip want to join us for a game? Yes, _____ .

5. Do you have a piano lesson on Fridays? No, _____ .

6. Were you all pleased with your results? Yes, _____ .

7. Are the girls making tea? Yes, _____ .

8. Am I talking too loudly? Yes, _____ .

9. Did you hear that funny noise? 'Yes, _____ .

10. Has the rain stopped? Yes, _____ .

11. Is Peter going to be in the team? No, _____ .

12. Have you found your handphone? 'No, _____ .

13. Did you enjoy your visit to Britain? 'Yes, _____ .

14. Was Jane late for her violin lesson? No, _____ .

Answering Questions

■ You can use pronouns + **be**, **have** and **do** by themselves to answer questions:

'**Are** you **going** to the match?' 'No, **I'm** not.'

'**Have** you **got** enough room?' 'Yes, thanks, **I have**.'

'**Do** you **like** strawberries?' 'Yes, **I do**.'

Agreeing

■ You can use pronouns + **be**, **have** and **do** in the same way to agree with statements:

Helen **has** lovely hair.
Yes, she **has**.

It**'s** too late to begin now.
Yes, it **is**.

Dan **plays** the violin very well.
Yes, he **does**.

B **Complete the short agreements in the following exercise:**

1. George performed very well in the play. Yes, _____he did_____ .

2. I think I've made a mistake. Yes, _____you have_____ .

3. Dad's very late home this evening. Yes, _____ .

4. Mum makes delicious desserts. Yes, _____ .

5. I suppose all the tickets are already sold. Yes, _____ .

6. The Browns have probably moved house. Yes, _____ .

7. The weather is improving a bit. Yes, _____ .

8. This room looks very untidy. Yes, _____ .

9. Miss Lee always wears smart clothes. Yes, _____ .

10. That was an excellent match! Yes, _____ .

11. She gave up too quickly. Yes, _____ .

12. Jim's likely to win the high jump again. Yes, _____ .

13. I worked very hard last term. Yes, _____ .

14. Those two colours go together quite well. Yes, _____ .

Negative Question Tags

- You use question tags to ask people to agree with what you have just said.

- You use negative question tags after positive statements: You like skating, **don't** you?

- A sentence beginning **There is** (or **are, was, were**) needs **there** in the question tag: **There are** plenty of pencils, **aren't there**?

C Add a question tag after each of the following statements:

1. I'm taller than you are, _____aren't I_____ ?

2. That was an interesting programme, _____wasn't it_____ ?

3. The bus leaves at 7.15, _____ ?

4. The flowers look lovely on the table, _____ ?

5. This is an excellent place for a swim, _____ ?

6. You've all got your own copies, _____ ?

7. There's another tablecloth in the cupboard, _____ ?

8. Squirrels eat nuts, _____ ?

9. Sophie made a beautiful bridesmaid, _____ ?

10. The mirror cracked from side to side, _____ ?

11. The hens have laid plenty of eggs today, _____ ?

12. The weather is going to clear up tomorrow, _____ ?

13. I suppose I'm too late for lunch now, _____ ?

14. We need some more chairs, _____ ?

Positive Question Tags

■ You use positive question tags after negative statements: You **don't** like football, **do** you?

D **Add positive question tags after the following statements:**

1. These spectacles don't belong to Grandad, <u>*do they*</u> ?

2. You haven't made your bed yet, <u>have you</u> ?

3. That film wasn't very good, _____ ?

4. Freddie didn't win the drawing competition, _____ ?

5. These trees aren't fully grown yet, _____ ?

6. You didn't turn the light off, _____ ?

7. We don't have any bread, _____ ?

8. You haven't got a computer of your own, _____ ?

9. This train doesn't go to Melaka, _____ ?

10. Jill and I aren't in the swimming team, _____ ?

11. Granny and Grandad didn't stay very long, _____ ?

12. It's not my fault if the bus is late, _____ ?

13. There aren't enough rolls for breakfast, _____ ?

14. You don't need these old file boxes, _____ ?

15 THE HELPING VERBS *SHALL* AND *WILL*: THE FUTURE

A Fill in **will** or **shall** in the following sentences; use **shall** for **I** and **we**, and use **won't** and **shan't** where you can:

Shall or Will?

- You can use **shall** or **will** with **I** and **we**.
- You use **will** with **you, he, she, it, they**, and with plural or singular nouns.
- You can shorten **shall not** to **shan't** and **will not** to **won't**.

1. I _____shan't_____ ~~not~~ be able to meet you at the station.

2. This colour _____ go better with your curtains.

3. We _____ all miss our cousins when they go home.

4. I hope you _____ not be late tonight.

5. The new ring road _____ make a big difference to the city-centre traffic.

6. The senior school _____ feel strange at first.

7. It _____ not be long before the baby's walking.

8. _____ you see Janet later today?

9. My brother and I _____ arrange accommodation for you.

10. Everybody _____ want to read the new Harry Potter book.

11. We _____ not be upset if we don't win.

12. I _____ send you your tickets — there _____ not be any problems.

13. The dictionary _____ not be published till September.

14. That bed _____ break if you jump on it like that.

15. _____ I start the washing machine?

16. The computer _____ not work if you don't turn it on.

Question Tags with Shall and Will

■ *You can shorten the personal pronouns + will to: **I'll, you'll, he'll, she'll, it'll, we'll, they'll**.*

B In the following exercise, fill in the gaps in the main sentence or the question tag with **will, shall, won't** or **shan't**.

Match **shall** with **shan't**, but match **will** or the short forms on the left with **won't**.

1. We shall be late if we don't hurry, ___shan't___ we?

2. You ___won't___ tell anybody, will you?

3. They'll catch us up soon, _____ they?

4. I shan't see you till Friday, _____ I?

5. It _____ be necessary to change our money, will it?

6. We shan't reach home till after midnight, _____ we?

7. You'll be glad when your exam is over, _____ you?

8. There _____ be any problem over the air tickets, will there?

9. Your parents will be able to come to the school play, _____ they?

10. Susie _____ make a lovely bridesmaid, won't she?

11. Jenny and I shall get to the top of the hill first, _____ we?

12. I'll be able to contact you on your handphone, _____ I?

13. You won't give away the secret, _____ you?

14. We'll see you at the party later, _____ we?

C Fill in the future continuous form of the verb in the following sentences. Use short forms wherever you can. You can choose whether to use **will** or **shall** with **I** and **we**.

Future Continuous

■ You often use the future continuous (**will** or **shall** + **be** + present participle) instead of just **will** or **shall** + base form, for example, you can say:

I **shan't be needing** these boxes

instead of

I **shan't need** those boxes.

1. We ____shan't____ ~~not~~ __be wanting__ these keys again. (**want**)

2. I expect you __'ll be meeting__ Miss Lee tomorrow. (**meet**)

3. Granny _____ not _____ till this evening. (**arrive**)

4. I _____ my exam results very soon. (**get**)

5. The new motorway _____ very soon. (**open**)

6. Mum and Dad _____ me from school today. (**collect**)

7. We _____ dinner at eight o'clock tonight. (**have**)

8. _____ you _____ a pharmacy on your way home? (**pass**)

9. I _____ not _____ on the school trip on Wednesday. (**go**)

10. The ship _____ at 5.15 this evening. (**sail**)

11. _____ I _____ you at the rehearsal tonight? (**see**)

12. The supermarket _____ in five minutes. (**close**)

13. We _____ French next term. (**start**)

14. James _____ not _____ in tomorrow's match. (**playing**)

D Complete the short answers in the following exercise:

Short Answers to Will/Shall or Going To?

■ You often use **be going to** instead of **shall** and **will** when you are talking about plans that have already been made: I'**m going to** get my hair cut tomorrow.

1. Is Harry going to come too? No, ____he isn't____ .

2. You'll remember, won't you? Yes, ____I will____ . (or ____I shall____)

3. Is there going to be barbecue tomorrow? Yes, _____ .

4. Shall I be disturbing you if I practise the piano?

No, _____ .

5. Are you going to enter for the design competition?

No, _____ .

6. Will this be your first trip abroad? Yes, _____ .

7. Are Philip and Harry going to buy the drinks?

Yes, _____ .

8. Won't the car start? No, _____ .

9. You won't forget to phone me, will you?

No, _____ .

10. Will there be a problem if I'm a bit late?

No, _____ .

11. Won't we be too late to get seats? No, _____ .

12. Won't your Mum be cross with you? Yes, _____ .

13. Aren't you going to lay the table? Yes, _____ .

14. Shall we be in your way if we play here?

No, _____ .

16 THE HELPING VERBS CAN, COULD, WOULD

A 1 Fill in **can** or **can't**, using the verb in brackets:

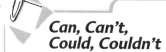

1. _____Can_____ you _____swim_____? Yes, I _____can_____. (**swim**)

2. I _____can run_____ but I _____can't dance_____. (**run, dance**)

3. _____ you _____? No, I _____. (**ski**)

4. Jim _____ and he _____, but he _____. (**draw, paint, sing**)

5. I'm afraid you _____ your car there. (**park**)

6. Where are my glasses? I _____ them. (**find**)

7. Don't shout. I _____ you perfectly well. (**hear**)

8. _____ you _____ the ceiling when you stretch up? Yes, I _____. (**touch**).

A 2 Fill in **could** or **couldn't**, using the verb in brackets:

1. The shelf was too high, so I _____couldn't reach_____ it. (**reach**)

2. I tried to phone you but I _____ your number. (**remember**)

3. When I opened the window I _____ the birds singing. (**hear**)

4. I was so excited that I _____. (**sleep**)

5. The view was wonderful. We _____ for miles. (**see**)

6. We _____ which apartment to choose, because we liked both. (**decide**)

7. I knew you _____ if you tried. (**win**)

8. Although I _____ my handphone ringing,

I _____ it. (**hear, find**)

B Fill in **could you, could I** or **can I**, using the verb in brackets.

1. Please _____could you move_____ your car? (**move**).

2. Please _____ me the sugar? (**pass**)

3. _____ two litres of milk, please? (**have**)

4. _____ me your e-mail address? (**give**)

5. _____ your newspaper? (**read**)

6. Please _____ your radio? (**turn off**)

7. _____ this bag for me? (**carry**)

8. _____ you a drink? (**get**)

9. Please _____ a cup of coffee? (**have**)

10. _____ your telephone? (**use**)

11. _____ me what time it is? (**tell**)

12. Please _____ more slowly? (**speak**)

C Fill in **would** or **wouldn't** + a verb from the box below. Use short forms wherever you can:

be	buy	enjoy	help	mend
obey	open	start	stop	~~work~~

1. I switched on the computer but it _____wouldn't work_____ .

2. Mum said she _____ me with my spelling.

3. We got into the car but it _____ .

60

4. Dad promised he _____ my bicycle.

5. Miss Lee was angry with Jane because she _____ talking.

6. I thought I _____ late so I began to run.

7. George _____ his dad, so he was punished.

8. We turned the handle, but the door _____ .

9. I asked Peter and Sue if _____ the drinks for the party.

10. I knew you _____ your holiday in London.

D **1** **Below are some answers, but the questions are missing. Can you complete the questions using would you like + one of the phrases from the box?**

a~~ cup of tea~~	a glass of juice
ice cream for dessert	some more noodles
to come shopping	to go today
to rest	to watch it

Would you like?

- You use **Would you like** to offer things: **Would you like** a drink?

- You also use **Would you like** to invite people to do things: **Would you like** to come to dinner this evening?

1. __Would you like a cup of tea__? Yes please, I'd love one.

2. Where _____ today? I'd like to go to the zoo.

3. You look tired. _____ now? Yes, I would.

4. I've got a new video. _____? Yes, I'd love to.

5. _____ with me this morning? I'm sorry, I can't - I'm busy this morning.

6. _____? I'd prefer a cup of coffee, if that's OK.

61

7. _____ ? Yes, I'd love that.

8. _____ ? No, thank you - I've had enough.

I would like

■ You use **I would like** to ask for something for yourself. You usually shorten **I would like** to **I'd like**.

D **2** **Say what you want to have or do, using I'd like + a phrase from the box. Remember you can say I'd love ... instead, in answer to an invitation:**

a boiled egg and some toast	a drink of water
to buy some stamps	to come to your party
to finish this bit of work	to go swimming
~~to go to bed~~	to leave at 7.30

1. I'm very tired.
   I'd like **to go to bed.**

2. Where's the post office?
   _____

3. I'm rather thirsty.
   _____

4. Is there a sports complex nearby?
   _____

5. Thank you for the invitation.
   _____

6. Could you wake me early?
   _____

7. What would you like for breakfast?
   _____

8. I'm busy just now.
   _____

17 THE HELPING VERBS MAY, MIGHT, MUST, SHOULD

A Complete the following questions, answers and statements, using the pronoun or name in brackets, and choosing a verb from the box below:

access	bring	come	go
have	park	play	put
stay	try	turn on	use

1. (**we**) _____May we park_____ our van here? No, _____you may not_____ .

2 (**Emma**) _____May Emma come_____ to dinner this evening? Yes, of course _____she may_____ .

3. (**you**) _____ your PC to school, but _____ it in the exam.

4. (**we**) _____ to the cinema now? No, _____ .

5. (**I**) _____ my e-mails from your computer? Yes, of course _____ .

6. (**Danny**) _____ dinner here, but _____ the night.

7 (**Carol**) _____ your exercise bike? Yes, _____ .

8. (**Tom**) _____ his CDs on this shelf? Yes, _____ .

9. (I) _____ the television? No,

_____ .

10. (Frankie and Harry) _____ football

with me? Yes, _____ .

May for Possibility

- You use **may** for possible or likely happenings: Take an umbrella. It **may rain**.

- You can also use **might** for possible or likely happenings: Take a jacket. It **might be** cold.

- You use **might** as the past tense of **may** or **might**: They said they **might arrive** on Friday.

B Choose a verb from the box below, and complete the following sentences. In this exercise, use **may** in the present tense:

be	break	enjoy	~~feel~~
find	get	~~go swimming~~	help
see	slip	spend	want

1. Bring your bathing costume. We __may go swimming__ .

2. I knew you __might feel__ hungry after your journey, so I've made you some supper.

3. I _____ Jack at the rehearsal tonight.

4. You _____ not _____ Malay too difficult to learn.

5. We thought you _____ this video.

6. There _____ a delay, so bring something to read.

7. Please bring the chairs indoors. They _____ wet.

8. Granny _____ a rest when she arrives.

9. I was afraid I _____ on the wet rocks.

10. If you ask me nicely, I _____ you solve the puzzle.

11. We _____ our vacation in New Zealand.

12. Careful with those eggs — you _____ them.

Must and Have To

- Use **must** if it is necessary to do something: We **must hurry**.

- You also use **must** if you are keen to do something, or if you are keen for someone else to do something: You **must read** this book. I **must see** that movie.

- The short form of **must not** is **mustn't**. Use **must not** or **mustn't** when something is not allowed: You **mustn't run** in the corridor.

- When something is not necessary, you can use **do not have to**: I **don't have to go** yet.

- You use **had to** as the past tense of **must**: I **had to run** to catch the bus. You can use **didn't have to** if something wasn't necessary: We **didn't have to queue** for tickets.

- But you can keep **must** as the past tense after a saying or thinking verb: I realized I **must work** hard. I knew I **mustn't show** that I was frightened.

C Fill in **must, mustn't, had to, don't have to** or **didn't have to**, choosing a verb from the box below:

alter	buy	catch	finish	forget
get up	have	leave	meet	open
tell	wait	wear	write	

1. I ___must catch___ the 7.30 train or I'll be late for my meeting.

2. Miss Lee found me a spare copy of the book, so I ___didn't have to buy___ one.

3. Dad told us he _____ some work for his boss.

4. I'm very tired — I _____ some sleep.

5. You _____ anything on my computer, because it will cause problems.

6. It's still early — we _____ yet.

7. You _____ me all about your trip.

8. I'm sorry I'm late — I _____ an hour for a bus.

9. You knew you _____ the school grounds without permission.

10. We _____ all our cases when we came through the customs.

11. You _____ clearly in your exam.

12. The weather was hot and dry in London, so we _____ our raincoats at all.

Should and Ought To

- You use **should** if it is right, or correct, or normal, or a good idea, to do something: You **should eat** plenty of vegetables.

- The short form of **should not** is **shouldn't**: You **shouldn't tell** lies.

- **Ought to** means the same as **should**: You **ought to be** able to spell your own name by now. You **ought not to** miss that movie.

D Fill in **should** or **shouldn't** in the following sentences, choosing a verb from the box below. Then write the sentence again using **ought to** or **ought not to**:

believe	eat	let	make
read	take	think	try

1. You ___should take___ more exercise.
   You ought to take more exercise.

2. We ___shouldn't believe___ everything we hear.
   We ought not to believe everything we hear.

3. You _____ the exam paper carefully before beginning to write.

   _____

4. Sally _____ more use of her acting talents.

   _____

5. You _____ to do so many things at once.

   _____

6. You _____ so much fatty food.

   _____

7. They _____ their dog's barking disturb the neighbours.

   _____

8. You _____ carefully before you decide.

   _____

18 MORE TENSES

Past Perfect

- The **past perfect** of any verb is formed with the helping verb **had** + past participle of the verb: He **had torn** his shirt. My handphone **had disappeared**.

- When you are using the **simple past** to say what **happened**, you use the **past perfect** to mention something that **happened before then**: I **got up** at eight o'clock and I **saw** that the mail **had arrived**. (If you were talking in the present tense, you'd say 'The mail **has arrived**.')

- You can shorten **I had, you had, he had, she had, we had, they had** to **I'd, you'd, he'd, she'd, we'd, they'd**: I didn't want to see the movie because **I'd seen** it before.

- You can shorten **had not** to **hadn't**: Mary **hadn't been feeling** well for some days.

A Complete these sentences using the past perfect tense + a verb from the box. Use shortened forms wherever you can.

~~arrange~~	bring	disappear	do
find	happen	leave	lose
rescue	see	take	turn

1. I met Susan at the bench in the park, as we ___'d arranged___ .

2. The two of us _____ not _____ each other for several weeks.

3. After I _____ a photograph I put my camera on the bench.

4. We talked about the things we _____ during the past few weeks.

5. We walked off, but I realized I _____ my camera on the bench.

6. When I got back to the bench, my camera _____ .

7. I told the park attendant that I _____ my camera.

8. He said a lady _____ a camera to the office a few minutes before.

9. I was very relieved that I _____ my camera.

10. I thanked the lady who _____ my camera from the bench.

11. I went home and told my mum what _____ in the park.

12 She was glad the day _____ not _____ out badly after all.

Future Perfect

■ You form the **future perfect** of any verb with **will** or **shall** + **have** + past participle of the verb: The plane **will have landed**. We **shall have arrived**.

■ You use the **future perfect** to say that a certain happening will be over by a certain time in the future: Good luck for your exam results. You **will have received** them by the time you get this letter. I **shall have started** my new job when I see you in January.

B Choose a verb from the box and use the future perfect to fill in the gaps in these sentences. Use shortened forms such as **he'll, we'll, won't, shan't** wherever you can:

arrive	have	~~hear~~	learn	open
recover	~~return~~	settle	start	wake

1. I _'ll have returned_____ to Singapore by the time you receive my postcard from London.

2. You ___won't___ ~~not~~ yet ___have heard___ that I've got a place at the university.

3. It's too early to phone them — they _____ not

    _____ up yet.

4. I expect you _____ into your new apartment by the time we see you again.

5. By this time tomorrow they _____ in Penang and will be enjoying the beaches.

6. I _____ not _____ time to go shopping, so we'll have to eat whatever is in the fridge.

7. _____ you already _____ your job at the hospital when we visit you in September?

8. Dad _____ from his cold by the time you come, so the baby won't catch it.

9. The hotel has been closed for months but it

   _____ again when all the tourists arrive.

10. By the age of 10, most children _____ to read, and will be enjoying lots of books.

C Choose a verb from the box, and fill in the gaps using the present perfect continuous. Use shortened forms such as **I've** or **he's** where you can:

cry	dig	do	exercise	hurry
learn	make	~~swim~~	try	use

1. Your hair is wet — ___*have*___ you _been swimming_ ?

2. The men _____ up the road, so there is a big hole in it.

3. You _____ that dress for weeks — isn't it finished yet?

4. _____ you _____ ? You look hot.

5. We _____ about orang utans at school.

6. What _____ you _____ since I saw you last?

7. _____ Jane _____ ? Her eyes look red.

8. I _____ to contact Peter on his handphone, without any success.

9. He _____ in the gym every morning, and he looks much fitter.

10. I can't find my handphone — who _____ it?

Past Perfect Continuous

- You form the **past perfect continuous** of any verb with **had** + **been** + the past participle of the verb: He **had been practising**, It **had been raining**.

- When you are using the **simple past** to say what **happened**, you use the **past perfect continuous** for continuous happenings and activities **before then**: When I moved to the senior school, **I had been learning** English for five years.

D Choose a verb from the box, and use the past perfect continuous to fill the gaps. Use shortened forms wherever you can:

eat	garden	run	snow	study
train	~~travel~~	wait	wonder	work

1. We 'd been travelling _____ all day so we were very tired.

2. It _____ in the night, and the ground was all white.

3. My camera _____ fine until I dropped it.

4. I _____ how to contact James when he called me on my handphone.

5. George _____ hard and felt he was ready for the race.

6. Mum's hands were dirty because she

   _____ .

7. Harry _____ not _____ enough, so he failed his exam.

8. The program _____ on the computer for several hours and the task was nearly finished.

9. I started getting fat because I _____ the wrong sort of food.

10. The girls _____ not _____ very long when a bus came.

70

19 TRANSITIVE AND INTRANSITIVE

A Write down the verbs and say whether they are transitive or intransitive. If they are transitive, write down the object. Some sentences have more than one verb.

Find the Object

■ The verb in a sentence sometimes has an object, and sometimes has no object:

Dad walked in.

He shut **the door**.

In the first sentence, the verb **walked (in)** has no object. It is an **intransitive verb**.

In the second sentence the verb **shut** has the object **the door**. **Shut** is a **transitive verb**.

1. We sat and waited.

   sit- intransitive, wait - intransitive

2. Mum heated Dad's dinner in the microwave.

   heat – transitive – Dad's dinner

3. Dad climbed the ladder and fitted a new light bulb.

4. Where have you put my pencil-sharpener?

5. Are you coming with us?

6. Sue went out and bought three bottles of juice and some bread.

7. I just caught the train in time.

8. James left school when he was 16.

9. Have another sandwich.

10. You die if you don't eat or drink.

11. Turn left when you reach the supermarket.

12. Please talk quietly or you'll wake the baby.

Two Objects

■ Some transitive verbs can have two objects, a direct object and an indirect object. The indirect object comes before the direct object.

Mum gave **me** *two dollars.* The **direct object** of **give** is **two dollars** and the **indirect object** is **me**.

Miss Lee read **her pupils** *a story.* The **direct object** of **read** is **a story**, and the **indirect object** is **her pupils**.

B **Pick out the verb, the direct object and the indirect object. You can use V for verb, DO for direct object, and IO for indirect object:**

1. Mum is making Susie a party dress.

   make (V), Susie (IO), a party dress (DO)

2. Tell me the whole story.

3. Could you hand me that list?

4. Have you sent Granny a postcard yet?

5. James sang us his favourite song.

6. Helen gave everybody a piece of cake.

7. Charlie is building his rabbit a hutch.

8. George lent Peter his bicycle.

9. Anna played her teacher the new piano piece.

10. Read me the second question.

11. Please fetch me another pack of paper from the cupboard.

12. Jean is going to cook her friends a delicious meal.

C Below are some pairs of sentences. Pick a verb from the box below that can be used in both sentences, and fill in the correct form. Say whether the verb is transitive or intransitive. You can use (T) or (I).

Verbs that can be Transitive or Intransitive

■ Many verbs can be used with or without an object.

change	draw	lose	open
play	read	stand	watch

1a. Anna ___reads___ a few pages of her book before she goes to sleep. (T)

1b. We each have to ___read___ aloud in class every day.(I)

2a. Please _____ still while I comb your hair.

2b. I can't _____ people who boast.

3a. Suddenly the door _____ and in came Harry.

3b. Could you _____ the door for me, Peter?

4a. David is artistic — he _____ very well.

4b. Hannah has _____ a portrait of Helen.

5a. I sang while Mum _____ the piano.

5b. The baby was _____ happily with her toy.

6a. Last night we _____ a programme about zebras.

6b. _____ carefully as I do the experiment.

7a. Did you win the match? No, we _____ .

7b. Dad is always _____ his spectacles.

8a. Joe _____ the date on his calendar as soon as he gets up.

8b. People _____ as they get older.

D Make your own pairs of intransitive and transitive commands, using the verbs provided, and choosing a set of words from the box:

back to let the ambulance pass	hard if you want to do well
in time to the music	neatly for school
on this rope	plenty of fresh vegetables
slowly or you'll choke	the baby for me
this diagram carefully	this rhythm
twice round the block	with both hands on the handlebars
your arms as you walk	your bicycle carefully in the traffic
your dog every day	your eyes from side to side

1. eat (I) <u>Eat slowly or you'll choke.</u>

   (T) <u>Eat plenty of fresh vegetables.</u>

2. move (I) _____.

   (T) _____.

3. ride (I) _____.

   (T) _____.

4. dress (I) _____.

   (T) _____.

5. walk (I) _____.

   (T) _____.

6. clap (I) _____.

   (T) _____.

7. swing (I) _____.

   (T) _____.

8. study (I) _____.

   (T) _____.

20 THE PASSIVE

Making Verbs Passive

■ You can turn a sentence with a transitive verb around, so that the object of the verb becomes its subject. When you do this, you make the verb **passive**:

ACTIVE: Jenny **took** this photograph.

PASSIVE: *This photograph* **was taken** *by Jenny.*

■ You form the **simple present passive** of any verb with **am, is** or **are** + past participle of the verb: The rubbish **is removed** by the dustmen.

■ You form the **simple past passive** of any verb with **was** or **were** + past participle of the verb: The piece **was composed** by Mozart at the age of ten.

A Turn the following sentences around into the passive:

1. Anna takes the children to the park every afternoon.

   The children are taken to the park by Anna every day.

2. Sir Christopher Wren designed St Paul's Cathedral.

   _____

3. Vincent played the part of the wicked uncle.

   _____

4. Wordsworth wrote this poem.

   _____

5. The caretaker opens the school at 8.00.

   _____

6. Mr Kwo trains the football team.

   _____

7. A bee stung me on the arm.

   _____

8. Sir Stamford Raffles founded Singapore.

_____

9. My grandfather collected these books.

_____

10. The government owns this apartment block.

_____

11. In 1941 a bomb destroyed the house.

_____

12. A taxi knocked me off my bike.

_____

Prepositions used with the Passive

- The prepositions **in** and **with** are used with passive verbs, as well as **by**.

- The preposition **in** is often used after verbs that mean cover, such as **dress, clothe, wrap**.

- The preposition **with** is often used after verbs that mean fill, such as **stuff, crowd, cram**.

B Form passive sentences in the simple past with the words in brackets. Decide whether to use **by, in** or **with** after the passive verb:

1. (My boots, cover, mud)

   My boots were covered in mud.

2. (The valley, form, ice)

   The valley was formed by ice.

3. (Mum's present, wrap, coloured paper)

   _____

4. (The street, crowd, people)

   _____

5. (The seeds, carry, wind)

   _____

6. (The prince, clothe, fine robes)

   _____

7. (Maggie's wardrobe, cram, clothes)

   _____

8. (The ship, hit, torpedo)

_____

9. (The air, fill, strange noises)

_____

10. (The damage, cause, a hurricane)

_____

11. (Sue, dress, purple)

_____

12. (The drawer, cram, papers)

_____

More Tenses in the Passive

- ■ You form the **present passive continuous** of any verb with **am, is** or **are** + **being** + past participle of the verb: I'**m being taught** dancing by Miss Wu.
- ■ You form the **past passive continuous** of any verb with **was** or **were** + **being** + past participle of the verb: The timetable **was being prepared** by the head teacher.
- ■ You form the **future passive** with **will** or **shall** + **be** + past participle of the verb: The goods **will be posted** to you tomorrow.
- ■ You form the **present perfect passive** of any verb with **have** + **been** + past participle of the verb: The goods **have been sent** by first-class mail.
- ■ You form the **past perfect passive** of any verb with **had** + **been** + past participle of the verb: The floor **had been swept**.

C Turn the following active sentences into passive sentences:

1. The police will remove any vehicles parked outside the air terminal.

   Any vehicles parked outside the air terminal will be

   removed by the police.

2. The picnickers had dropped a lot of litter.

   _____

3. The mechanic has repaired the car.

   _____

4. The police were towing away our van.

   _____

5. My dad is teaching my brother to drive.

   _____

6. A mole has made those bumps in the lawn.

   _____

7. Mary will read the part of the First Ugly Sister.

   _____

8. Computers have completely changed our lives.

   _____

9. The pupils are making the scenery for the play.

   _____

10. The builders had left some rubbish in the drive.

    _____

11. The head teacher's daughter is presenting the prizes.

    _____

12. A catering firm will provide refreshments.

    _____

- When a passive verb is used, there is often no mention of the person or thing that does the action, because it isn't important to mention them: The workmen **haven't been paid** yet. We **were asked** for our opinions. **Has** the tap **been repaired**?

- In the active form of these sentences the subject could be something like **they** or **we** or **somebody** or **anybody**: **We** haven't paid the workmen yet. **They** asked us for our opinions. Has **anybody** repaired the tap?

- You can change an active sentence that begins with something like **They say** or **People think** or **No-one knows** into the passive like this, using **it** as the subject: **It is said**, **It is thought**, **It isn't known**: **It isn't known** how the accident happened. **It is believed** that the driver fell asleep.

D **1**   **Change these active sentences into passives, without mentioning the doer of the action:**

1.   We haven't sent in our competition entry yet.

   Our competition entry hasn't been sent in yet.

2.   They told the passengers that the train was running late.

   _____

3.   They asked us to wait in a queue.

   _____

4.   Have they mended the lamp post?

   _____

5.   Somebody left these papers on the table.

   _____

6.   They ordered the prisoners to go back to their cells.

   _____

7.   Has anybody cleaned the bedrooms?

   _____

8.   They serve dinner between six o'clock and nine o'clock.

   _____

D **2** **Change these active sentences into passives, using it as the subject:**

1. People now believe that the universe began with a big bang.

   It is now believed that the universe began with a big bang.

   _____

2. They say that eating a lot of eggs is bad for you.

   _____

   _____

3. Nobody knows who invented the wheel.

   _____

   _____

4. People believe that holidays help you to relax.

   _____

   _____

5. They think that the illness comes from eating rotten fruit.

   _____

   _____

6. We know that the stars are getting further apart.

   _____

   _____

7. They say that a good education is the key to success.

   _____

   _____

8. They believe that the man was murdered.

   _____

   _____

21 MORE PRACTICE WITH QUESTION TAGS

A Add a question tag at the end of the following sentences:

1. People should be careful not to hurt each other's

   feelings, ___*shouldn't they*___ ?

2. Your sister has completed her training as a teacher,

   ___*hasn't she*___ ?

3. You won't forget to buy the sausages,

   _____ ?

4. Medical students have to work very hard,

   _____ ?

5. James could walk when he was only eight months old,

   _____ ?

6. There's a pharmacy in the next street, _____ ?

7. Mum wanted to buy some more CDs, _____ ?

8. It's too late to telephone them, _____ ?

9. David hadn't started French before he went to college, _____ ?

10. You were only pretending, _____ ?

11. We mustn't lose the tickets, _____ ?

12. Your parents are going to come with us, _____ ?

B **Add question tags to the following sentences:**

1. There wouldn't be a problem about changing the tickets, ____would there____ ?

2. You could buy an exercise bike, _____ ?

3. Sheila must enjoy looking after old people, _____ ?

4. David and I could go on ahead, _____ ?

5. It would be a good idea to warn them, _____ ?

6. Jean could start frying the steaks now, _____ ?

7. Bill would make a good team captain, _____ ?

8. There must be a good explanation, _____ ?

9. The children could travel a day earlier, _____ ?

10. They wouldn't need the room for more than a week, _____ ?

C Add question tags after these sentences:

1. The ambulance couldn't have got here any sooner, ____could it____ ?

2. They would have told us if their plans had changed, _____ ?

3. The thunderstorm must have caused the computer to crash, _____ ?

4. You could have tidied your room, _____ ?

5. In those days they would have hanged people for stealing, _____ ?

6. I should have sent you a text message, _____ ?

7. We'll have cycled 200 kilometres by the end of the holiday, _____ ?

8. It wouldn't have been fair to punish them, _____ ?

9. It must have rained very hard in the night, _____ ?

10. She could have won if she'd tried harder, _____ ?

When there are two Helping Verbs

■ There are sometimes two or even three helping verbs in a sentence. For example, when you are talking about a past situation, you often use **have** after the first helping verb: You should **have** warned me. I could **have** helped you. You must **have** made a mistake.

■ When you put a question tag after a sentence with two or more helping verbs, use only the first one in the question tag: The workmen **will have** finished by the weekend, **won't** they?

Passives and Continuous Tenses

■ Passive verbs often have two helping verbs: My clothes **are being** washed. The dishes **have been** washed. You only use the first one in the question tag: My clothes **are** being washed, **aren't** they? The dishes **have** been washed, **haven't** they?

■ Some continuous tenses have two helping verbs: They **have been** trying to contact us. The question tag only uses the first: They **had been** cheating, **hadn't** they?

D Add question tags after these sentences. They don't all have two helping verbs:

1. The book was being turned into a film, ___wasn't it___ ?

2. Breakfast is served between 7.30 and 10.00, ___isn't it___ ?

3. Jack was ordered to apologize, _____ ?

4. John has already been working in the hospital for some months, _____ ?

5. The wedding is being videoed, _____ ?

6. The book was never published, _____ ?

7. This film will be finishing soon, _____ ?

8. They had been looking for an apartment for ages, _____ ?

9. You've been trained as a teacher, _____ ?

10. The office had been closed for a month, _____ ?

22 -ING NOUNS AND TO-INFINITIVES

A Fill in the gaps with a verbal noun formed from one of the verbs in the box:

arrive	bake	brush	climb
cry	do	get	go
rain	tidy	~~wait~~	work

1. I can't stand _____waiting_____ in a queue.

2. Jean enjoys _____ cakes.

3. Mum suggested _____ out for dinner.

4. Barry loves _____ mountains.

5. I never mind _____ hard.

6. Have you finished _____ your room?

7. Peter tried _____ his teeth with soap.

8. It has stopped _____ at last.

9. Dad can't bear _____ the shopping.

10. I hate _____ late for anything.

11. Joe likes _____ up early.

12. The baby woke up and started _____ .

-ing Nouns

- The **-ing** form of verbs (run**ning**, walk**ing**, fight**ing**) is often used as a noun, called a **verbal noun** or **gerund**: **Exercising** regularly is good for you. No **parking** is allowed in the hospital grounds.

- These verbal nouns or gerunds are often used as the object of another verb: I **enjoy cycling**. He never **stops complaining**.

B Fill in the gaps with a *to*-infinitive using the verbs in the box:

~~come~~	hold	hurt	leave	listen
meet	rain	sing	take	train
travel	walk	write		

1. Do you want _____to come_____ to the shops with me?

2. You don't need _____ yet — it's not late.

to-infinitives

- Many verbs can be followed by **to** + the infinitive (the base form) of another verb: He **decided to leave** school early. Granny **learnt to use** a computer very quickly.

3. Don't forget _____ your umbrella with you.

4. My parents are planning _____ abroad.

5. I didn't mean _____ your feelings.

6. Joe hopes _____ as a doctor.

7. Mum has arranged _____ the head teacher next week.

8. The birds woke me up when they began _____ .

9. We intended _____ a barbecue, but it started

   _____ .

10. Has the baby learnt _____ yet?

11. I'm trying _____ to the radio.

12. I promise _____ to you every week.

-ing form or to-infinitive?

Here are some useful notes:

■ *You use only an **-ing** form with these verbs: **enjoy, finish, mind, stand, stop, suggest**.*

■ *You use only a **to**-infinitive with these verbs: **decide, expect, forget, hope, learn, need, offer, plan, promise, refuse, want**.*

■ *You can use either an **-ing** form or a **to**-infinitive with these verbs: **bear, begin, continue, hate, like, love, prefer, start**.*

■ *BUT:*

   (1) *if you use **would like, would hate, would love,** you need a **to**-infinitive, not an **-ing** form:* Bob **would hate to cause** trouble. I'**d love to come** with you.

   (2) *the verb **try** is followed by a **to**-infinitive when it means to attempt, but you use an **-ing** form when **try** means to do something to see what it's like:* Have you ever **tried putting** pepper on strawberries? I **tried to open** the door.

C Fill in the gaps with an **-ing** form or a **to**-infinitive formed from a verb in the box:

carry	drive	eat	fix	listen
miss	practise	return	sleep	spend
take	~~travel~~	walk	write	

1. I prefer _____travelling_____ (or _____to travel_____) by train.

2. Would you like _____ a shower now?

3. Dad tried _____ the car by himself but he didn't succeed.

4. I can't bear _____ scales on the piano.

5. The taxi-driver refused _____ my luggage up the stair.

6. I'll call you back — I haven't finished _____ my dinner yet.

7. I'd hate _____ any of the fun.

8. Some pupils continued _____ after they'd been told to put their pens down.

9. Sam offered _____ us to the station.

10. I've never tried _____ out of doors without a tent.

11. Chris enjoys _____ on his own in the hills.

12. Sue suggested _____ the morning in the museum.

13. Don't forget _____ the keys to the hotel staff.

14. Mum likes _____ to the radio whiles she irons the clothes.

More uses of a to-infinitive

- You can use a **to**-infinitive after many adjectives: The dancers were **lovely to watch**. Is that fruit **good to eat**?

- You often use a **to**-infinitive after nouns and after the pronouns **something, anything, nothing**: I always take **a book to read** on the train. I don't have **anything to wear** for the party.

D Fill in the gaps with an adjective, noun or pronoun from the top box, and a **to**-infinitive formed with a verb from the lower box:

afraid	anything	difficult	exciting
nice	nothing	something	space
tasks	uncomfortable	unlikely	~~welcome~~

ask	~~come~~	complete	do
drink	eat	park	pass
read	see	sit	watch

1. You are very ___welcome to come___ to my party on Friday.

2. The stone step was rather _____ on.

3. Children get bored when they have _____ all day.

4. The island was _____ because of the fog.

5. Those nuts are not very _____ — they taste bitter.

6. Don't be _____ questions in class.

7. Did you find a _____ the car in?

8. You're _____ your exam if you do no work.

9. These exercises give you various _____ .

10. I didn't have _____ so I borrowed Harry's computer magazine.

11. The match was very _____ .

12. You must be thirsty — I expect you'd like

    _____ .

23 ADVERBS (1)

A Choose an adjective from the box and turn it into an adverb to fill the gaps in these sentences:

angry	bright	brisk	careful
clear	comfortable	easy	~~gentle~~
gradual	loud	musical	neat
quiet	sudden		

1. Mum laid the baby ___gently___ in his cot.

2. Write your name _____ at the top of the page.

3. You're talking too _____ . Please speak _____ .

4. Carry those dishes very _____ .

5. If you're all sitting _____ , I'll begin the story.

6. The man shook his fist _____ at us.

7. Diana plays the piano very _____ .

8. Laura is a clever girl and passes all her exams _____ .

9. It happened so _____ that we all got a surprise.

10. The clouds _____ disappeared and the sun began to shine _____ .

11. Miss Lee was walking _____ across the playground.

12. Say your name _____ so that we can all hear what it is.

Formation of Adverbs

■ Adverbs belong with the verb of a sentence, and often describe it: She coughed **noisily.**

■ A lot of adverbs end in **–ly**. You form them by adding **-ly** to adjectives, for example: brave, brave**ly**, beautiful, beautiful**ly**.

■ But remember that adjectives ending in **-y** change **y** to **i** before **–ly**, for example, noisy, nois**ily**.

■ Adjectives that end with **-le** after another consonant, just add **y**: double, doub**ly**.

The -ly ending

- Not all words that end in **-ly** are adverbs. Some are adjectives.

- Some **-ly** words are both adjective and adverb, for example: *a **monthly** magazine (adjective); The magazine appears **monthly** (adverb).*

B **Say whether the bold word in the following sentences is an adverb or an adjective:**

1. Miss Lee's pupils are all very **lively**. ___*adjective*___

2. The hospital staff treated us very **kindly**. _____

3. Joe shook hands **politely** with his dad's boss.

   _____

4. That's a **lovely** bunch of flowers. _____

5. I was rather **lonely** when I first went to my new school.

   _____

6. The rubbish bins are emptied **weekly**. _____

7. Grandad complains that he is getting very **elderly**.

   _____

8. Sue had a cold and **wisely** decided to stay at home.

   _____

9. A **ghostly** shape moved across the room. _____

10. Please stand in an **orderly** queue. _____

11. Do you buy a **daily** newspaper? _____

12. The plant contains a poison that is **deadly** to cattle.

    _____

13. I **fully** understand your problems. _____

14. Our new neighbours are nice and **friendly**. _____

C **Decide which of the two forms is the correct one to fill the gap in the sentence:**

1. The exams are drawing ___*near*___ . (**near/nearly**)

2. I can _____ hear what you're saying. (**hard/ hardly**)

3. Have you seen Philip _____? (**late/lately**)

4. You've all worked _____, and you've done

   _____ in the test. (**hard/hardly, good/well**)

5. Thank you — you have been _____ helpful. (**most/mostly**)

6. I _____ forgot to take my key with me. (**near/nearly**)

7. I arrived _____ for my piano lesson. (**late/lately**)

8. Bob finished _____ in the race. (**last/lastly**)

9. I'm glad your parents are both _____. (**good/well**)

10. Don't worry — you're doing _____. (**fine/finely**)

11. Our pupils are _____ Chinese. (**most/mostly**)

12. Joe was _____ punished for his rudeness. (**just/justly**)

Adverbs without -ly

- Some adjectives can also be adverbs, for example, **hard, fast, late, early**:

  They work **hard** (adverb). This chair is rather **hard**. (adjective)

- There are sometimes two forms of adverb, one like the adjective, and one ending in **-ly**, but the two forms have different meanings, for example:

  He has **just** gone. They have been treated **justly**.

- Remember that the adverb for **good** is **well**:

  The children were **good**. They behaved **well**.

But **well** is also an adjective: I hope you are **well**.

Types of Adverb

- Many adverbs are single words, and many end in **-ly**, like the ones in the exercises above. But some adverbs consist of more than one word, for example, some adverbs of place and time: My desk is **over there**. I'll see you **next week**. These can be called **adverbial phrases**.

- There are many types of adverb. Here are some important types:

  manner: They treated us **fairly**.

  place or direction: Sometimes we have lessons **out of doors**. The sun is going **down**. I've looked **everywhere**.

  time: Have you finished **already**? It rained **last night**.

  frequency: We have a test **every week**. **Always** tell me if you're going out.

  duration: We have been waiting **for three hours**. The street is **temporarily** closed.

  emphasizing (used before adjectives, or before other adverbs): That's a **pretty** silly remark. I played **very** badly. These sums are **too** difficult for me.

  interrogative (asking a question): **How** did you do that? **Why** are you so upset? **Where** have you been?

D Fill the gaps with an adverb or adverbial phrase from the box that belongs to the type in brackets:

absolutely	~~all night~~	along the street
fast	for three weeks	how
into the bin	just	never
outside	rudely	severely
slowly	when	yet

1. The baby was crying ___all night___ . (**duration**)

2. Jack and I are going _____ to play football. (**place or direction**)

3. He was walking _____ _____ with a stick. (**manner, place**)

4. _____ is your brother taking his driving test? (**interrogative**)

5. Are you _____ sure you locked the door? (**emphasizing**)

6. _____ do that again! (**frequency**)

7. Have you done your homework _____ ? (**time**)

8. We shall be working on this project _____ . (**duration**)

9. Take this rubbish and put it _____ . (**place or direction**)

10. I've _____ heard the good news — congratulations! (**time**)

11. If you answer _____ like that I shall punish you _____ . (**manner, manner**)

12. _____ did you get here so _____ ? (**interrogative, manner**)

24 ADVERBS (2)

■ There are some adverbs, for example, **much, far, long**, that are used mainly in negative sentences (sentences containing words like **not** or **never**), or in questions, or with adverbs such as **hardly, rarely, seldom**: *Granny doesn't go into town* **much**. *Did you walk* **far**? *You rarely have to wait* **long** *for a bus*.

■ In positive sentences, instead of **much** you can use **a lot**; instead of **far** you use **a long way**; instead of **long** you use **a long time** or **for a long time**: *Granny goes into town* **a lot**. *We walked* **a long way**. *You have to wait* **a long time** *for a bus*.

A Use one of the expressions from the box to fill the gaps:

a long time	a long way	a lot
far	long	much

1. Kate lives ____a long way____ from her school.

2. We had not travelled _____ when we saw the mountains ahead of us.

3. The twins seem to quarrel _____ .

4. Have you been waiting _____ ?

5. I don't think the head teacher likes me _____ .

6. I haven't known Mary _____ , but I like her _____ .

7. We're still _____ from home.

8. Mr Brown has heart trouble and never walks _____ .

9. We had to queue _____ for tickets.

Emphasizing Adverbs

■ People use emphasizing adverbs to say how much an adjective or adverb is right for something or someone. For example, if you are thinking generally about the size of animals, you can say: An ant is **extremely** small. A cow is **rather** large. A rhinoceros is **very** large. An elephant is **extremely** large.

B Use an emphasizing adverb in the box with the adverb **well** or **badly** to say how each child did in the test:

fairly	quite	rather	very	extremely

well	badly

1. Maggie got 1 out of 10. She did ___extremely badly___ .

2. Dave got 7 out of 10. He did ___quite well___ .

3. Sally got 4 out of 10. She did _____ .

4. Joe got 5 out of 10. He did _____ .

5. Harry got 2 out of 10. He did _____ .

6. Mary got 9 out of 10. She did _____ .

7. Kate got 3 out of 10. She did _____ .

8. Kenneth got 6 out of 10. He did _____ .

9. Clever Laura got 10 out of 10. She did _____ .

10. Mary got 8 out of 10. She did _____ .

Sentence Adverbs

■ People often use adverbs like **fortunately, luckily, unfortunately, unluckily** at the beginning of a sentence to give their own comment on a situation: I arrived late at the station. **Fortunately** the train was still waiting.

C Write out the second sentence adding **fortunately** or **unfortunately**:

1. Thank you for the invitation to your party. I'll be away that day.

   Unfortunately I'll be away that day.

2. I ran as hard as I could to the bus stop. The bus hadn't left.

   _____

3. George cut his leg when we were out walking. I had some bandages in my pack.

   _____

4. We decided to take the coast road. We found that it was blocked by an accident.

   _____

5. It was Dad's birthday yesterday. I'd remembered to buy him a card.

   _____

6. I made a spelling mistake in my essay. Miss Lee didn't notice it.

   _____

7. I bought some eggs at the supermarket. I dropped them on the way home.

   _____

8. We were going to have a barbecue last night. It started to rain heavily.

   _____

9. I've been selected to play in Saturday's match. I've hurt my ankle.

   _____

10. The baby fell out of her cot. She wasn't hurt.

   _____

Adverbs in Middle Position

- Adverbs often come after the verb: You performed **brilliantly.** Adverbs can also begin a sentence: **Suddenly** there was a loud bang. But there is a group of adverbs that come in a special position in the middle of the sentence, before the verb: I **always** go for a run before breakfast. Susie **still** loves her teddy bear.

  Some important adverbs of this kind are: **already, also, always, ever, just, never, often, only, rarely, seldom, sometimes, still, usually.**

- There are also three important pronouns that can behave like adverbs and come in middle position. They are: **all, both, each:** We **each** read a passage aloud. They **all** passed.

- If there is a helping verb, these adverbs come between the helping verb and the main verb: Joe **was only trying** to help. We**'ve just heard** the news. **Do** you **ever come** to London? **Were** you **both born** in Japan?

- If the main verb is **be,** these adverbs come after it: The street **is often** full of traffic.

D Write these sentences adding the words in brackets in the correct position:

1. We don't visit the seaside. (**often**)

    We don't often visit the seaside.

2. Susan has worked hard at school. (**always**)

3. The twins want to become doctors. (**both**)

4. Mary had laid the table. (**already**)

5. The plane has landed. (**just**)

6. They received a copy of the rules. (**each**)

7. My parents travel abroad. (**sometimes**)

8. Dad comes home before eight o'clock. (**rarely**)

9. I've thought about you. (**often**)

10. Dave knew the answer. (**also**)

11. We were pleased with our results. (**all**)

12. Do you watch television after dinner? (**usually**)

13. Are you working at the café? (**still**)

   _____

14. He replies to my e-mails. (**never**)

   _____

15. People don't tell you the complete truth. (**always**)

   _____

16. What do you have for breakfast? (**usually**)

   _____

25 COMPARISON

More, Most

■ Adverbs that end in -ly form their comparative and superlative with **more** and **most**:

> quickly
> **more** quickly
> most **quickly**

A Put in the comparative or superlative adverb formed from the adjective in brackets:

1. I could meet you ___more conveniently___ on Tuesday than on Monday. (**convenient**)

2. Light travels _____ than sound. (**quick**)

3. This soap sells the _____ of all our products. (**successful**)

4. I'm sure you could live _____ than you do. (**economical**)

5. I _____ beg your pardon. (**humble**)

6. It was the _____ made bit of furniture that I've ever seen. (**clumsy**)

7. I'll try to explain again _____ . (**simple**)

8. I can reach the shelf _____ now that I'm a bit taller. (**easy**)

9. You calculated the total _____ than I did. (**accurate**)

10. Which of you can get ready for bed the _____ ? (**speedy**)

B Put in the correct comparative or superlative form. Some of the adverbs are -ly adverbs.

1. Art was the ___least___ difficult of all my exams. (**little**)

2. Andrea got here _____ than we did. (**early**)

3. Joe jumped _____ than me in the long jump. (**far**)

4. Whose was the _____ written essay? (**imaginative**)

5. I've worked _____ this week than ever before. (**hard**)

6. Why do we always arrive _____ than anybody else? (**late**)

7. Charles had folded his clothes _____ than usual. (**tidy**)

8. You'll find that you can speak English _____ than you think. (**well**)

9. I made my ice lolly last the _____ . (**long**)

10. Your schooldays come to an end _____ than you expect. (**soon**)

11. I enjoy maths lessons _____ than I used to. (**much**)

12. Really! That competition was the _____ organized event I've ever attended. (**badly**)

Comparison of non-ly Adverbs: faster, fastest

■ Adverbs that do not end in -**ly** have -**er** and -**est** endings:

Harry ran **fast**. George ran **faster**. I ran the **fastest**.

They'll arrive **soon**. They arrived **sooner** than we expected.

■ These five adverbs have irregular comparatives and superlatives:

badly (worse, worst); **far** (farther, farthest, or further furthest), **little** (less, least), **much** (more, most), **well** (better, best).

C Complete the second sentence, forming a comparative from one of the adjectives or adverbs in the box. Add **much** if there is a big difference. Add **a bit** if there is only a small difference:

early	~~expensive~~	far	large	late
long	near	small	well	young

1. Brown's Hotel is $50 a night and Black's Hotel is $48.

    Brown's Hotel is __a bit more expensive__ than Black's Hotel.

2. I got 18 marks out of 20 and Harry got 9 out of 20.

    I did _____ than Harry.

Emphasizing Adverbs used with Comparatives: much better, a bit nicer

■ People often use adverbs such as **much, a lot, a bit, slightly** with comparative adjectives and adverbs: Paris is **much nicer** than London. Dave is **slightly older** than me.

3. Mum's 38 and Dad is 40.

   Mum's _____ than Dad.

4. Sally walked 10 kilometres and Maggie walked 11 kilometres

   Maggie walked _____ than Sally.

5. The red carpet measures 5 x 5 metres and the blue one 5 x 4.5 metres.

   The blue carpet is _____ than the red one.

6. Singapore has a population of 2 million and London has a population of 11 million.

   London has a _____ population than Singapore.

7. The moon is 380,000 kilometres away, and the sun is 150 million kilometres away.

   The moon is _____ than the sun.

8. Dad gets up at 5 o'clock and Mum get up at 7.30.

   Dad gets up _____ than Mum.

9. Sally's been at this school for 6 years and I've been here for 5½ years.

   Sally's been at this school _____ than me.

10. George arrived at 9.00 and Peter arrived at 11.30.

    Peter arrived _____ than George.

D For each of the following sentences, write another sentence using **as ... as**:

1. It's less sunny today than it was yesterday.

   It isn't as sunny today as it was yesterday.

2. Harry can run faster than me.

   I can't run as fast as Harry.

3. The Lees' apartment is bigger than our apartment.

4. Sally is less untidy than Mary.

5. I live nearer to the school than Kenneth.

6. Dad enjoys television more than Mum.

7. Judy is less shy than she used to be.

8. I weigh more than my sister.

9. Maths is more difficult than English.

10. I'm less keen on dancing than Helen.

More Than, Less Than and Not As ... As

■ People often use **not as ... as** instead of comparatives. You can say:

Peter is **taller than** George. Or: George is**n't as tall as** Peter.

Mum is **less busy than** she used to be. Or: Mum is**n't as busy as** she used to be.

26 PREPOSITIONS (1)

Prepositions show Position and Connection

■ You use prepositions to express such things as the position and connection: The cat sat **on** the mat. You learn things **from** books. Come and sit **by** me. The first month **of** the year is January.

A Write down the prepositions in these sentences; there are more than one in some sentences:

1. Humpty Dumpty sat on a wall. ____on____

2. Jack and Jill went up the hill. _____

3. Sing a song of sixpence. _____

4. September comes after August. _____

5. Monday comes before Tuesday. _____

6. A flock of geese flew over the house. _____

7. Keep on the pedestrian crossing when you walk across the road. _____

8. Granny is coming to stay with us on Saturday. _____

9. Jump into the car and we'll go to the shops. _____

10. The witch put a spell on the prince and turned him into a frog. _____

11. When we got to the junction we stopped at the traffic lights. _____

12. He can't walk without a stick. _____

13. You mustn't talk during the exam. _____

14. Turn to page 21 and look at the diagram. _____

15. Draw a portrait of the person sitting opposite you. _____

B Write down the prepositions and put their objects in brackets:

Prepositions have Objects

■ Prepositions are always followed by a noun, noun phrase or pronoun.

We drove across **Paris**.

We drove across **the old bridge**.

We drove across **it**.

■ The noun, noun phrase or pronoun that follows a preposition is its **object**.

1. Sheila walked up the stairs.

   up (the stairs)

2. Dave came through the door.

   _____

3. George bumped into me.

   _____

4. Dad is in Tokyo just now.

   _____

5. Give this package to Julia.

   _____

6. You all know the story of Cinderella.

   _____

7. Is this play by Shakespeare?

   _____

8. I'm playing against Peter in the finals.

   _____

9. We opened the box and found nothing in it.

   _____

10. I'm taller than Joe, but Dave is taller than me.

   _____

11. The ball bounced right over the wall.

   _____

12. Danny is always quarrelling with his brother.

   _____

13. Kate fetched a chair from the corner for Miss Lee.

_____

14. Look at this strange insect on my hand.

_____

Prepositions that are more than one Word

■ Many prepositions are just single short words, like **on**, **to**, **in**.

■ But some prepositions consist of two or more words, like **away from** and **on top of**.

C Choose one of the prepositions from the first box, and an object from the second box, to fill the gaps:

ahead of	all over	along with	as far as
away from	~~close to~~	in between	in front of
next to	on board	on to	on top of
out of	up to		

his shirt	me	my toes
~~the beach~~	the bookcase	the corner
the electric fence	the hotel	the others
the platform	the ship	us
you	your desks	

1. Our hotel is ___close to the beach___ .

2. The lamp is sitting _____ .

3. Take your atlases _____ .

4. Come and sit _____ .

5. Keep _____ .

6. Are all the passengers _____ ?

7. The train stopped and we stepped down _____ .

8. I've got some sand _____ .

9. The taxi is waiting _____ .

10. Julia accompanied me _____ .

11. A stranger came _____ and asked us the time.

12. Jack has spilt orange juice _____ .

13. George was walking a few metres _____ .

14. Bring a friend _____ to my party.

D Say whether the bold word in these sentences is a preposition or an adverb:

1. We came to a bridge and drove **across**. _adverb_

2. Tell me **about** your holiday. _____

3. The fence is high but I can just see **over** if I stand on tiptoe. _____

4. There's a lot of flu **about** just now. _____

5. Who is hiding **behind** the door? _____

6. Is the manager **in** today? _____

7. John climbed **over** the wall. _____

8. We've been driving **around** the country sightseeing. _____

9. I put my shoes **outside** the door. _____

10. There was nobody **around** when we called. _____

11. Don't run **across** the street. _____

12. We went **outside** to watch the fireworks. _____

13. I left my umbrella **behind** in the bus. _____

14. Everybody put a coin **in** the hat. _____

27 PREPOSITIONS (2)

Prepositions of Position and Direction

- ■ You use **in** for position and **into** for direction or movement: I was **in** my bedroom. Mum came **into** my bedroom.

- ■ You use **on** for position and **on to** for direction or movement: I was sitting **on** the wall. Lisa climbed **on to** the wall.

- ■ But a few verbs of movement, for example, **place** and **land**, are followed by **in** or **on**: I **placed** the watch **in** its case. A bird **landed on** my windowsill.

A Put in one of the prepositions **in, into, on** or **on to**:

1. Hannah pushed me _____*into*_____ the swimming pool.

2. How many apples are there _____ the bowl?

3. The cat jumped _____ my bed.

4. We stood _____ the stage ready to sing.

5. I threw the rubbish _____ the bin.

6. Your spectacles are _____ the bathroom shelf.

7. The class marched _____ the hall for assembly.

8. The plane landed safely _____ the runway.

9. The cattle were led _____ the field.

10. I placed the vase of flowers _____ the table.

11. The team ran out _____ the football pitch.

12. The children are fast asleep _____ bed.

■ You often use the nouns **school**, **home**, **bed** with a preposition without **the**: I'm **in bed**. Get **out of bed**. Is your mum **at home?** Dave has gone **to school**, The children are **at school**.

■ If you walk somewhere you can say that you go there **on foot**: I go to school **on foot**.

■ You use the preposition **by** without **the** before nouns for forms of transport, such as **plane**, **car**, **train**, **bus**, **ship**: We're going to Kuala Lumpur **by plane**.

■ But if you put **the** before these transport nouns, or a determiner such as **my**, **his**, **this**, or a possessive such as **Mum's**, **Miss Lee's**, you use the prepositions **on** or **in**, not **by**: I go to school **on the bus**. I go to school **in Dad's car**.

■ You can travel or send goods **by air, by sea, by road, by rail**.

B **Put in the right preposition:**

1. We learn something new every day ____*at*____ school.

2. I usually travel to Granny's house _____ bus.

3. Granny usually brings me home _____ her car.

4. How do you travel _____ school in the mornings?

5. I go _____ tram to George Street, and I go the rest of the way _____ foot.

6. Melanie usually comes _____ school _____ bicycle.

7. The baby was already _____ bed when I got home _____ school.

8. I like travelling _____ the train, because I can read my book.

9. Most of our furniture is being sent _____ sea.

10. I saw Caroline going past _____ her bicycle.

11. There are special containers for transporting goods _____ rail.

12. The journey to Melaka _____ the bus took several hours.

Prepositions of Time

Here is Harry's timetable for today, Tuesday:

MORNING

8.30	Assembly.
9.00	Maths.
9.30	English.
10.00	Piano lesson.
10.45	Break.
11.00	Computer studies.
12.00	Gym.
1.00	Lunch.

AFTERNOON

2.10	History.
2.40	Geography.
3.10	Singing.
4.15	End of lessons.

C **Remind Harry what he has to do:**

1. You have Assembly ____*at*____ eight-thirty ____*in*____ the morning.

2. _____ Tuesdays, you have Maths _____ Assembly.

3. Your maths lesson lasts _____ half an hour.

4. Then you have English _____ nine-thirty _____ ten.

5. Your piano lesson is _____ ten o'clock.

6. Your piano lesson is the last lesson _____ Break.

7. _____ Break you have Computer studies _____ a whole hour.

8. Then it's Gym _____ midday, and lunch _____ one o'clock.

9. _____ the afternoon, _____ ten _____ two, you have History.

10. Then it's Geography _____ twenty _____ three _____ ten _____ three.

11. _____ that there's your Singing lesson _____ quarter _____ four.

12. Remember to do your homework _____ the evening.

108

D Choose a preposition from the box to fill the gaps in each sentence. You will have to use some prepositions more than once:

against	at	by	except	for
in	instead of	like	of	on
with	without			

1. I've bought a nice present _____for_____ Mum's birthday.

2. Are you playing _____ the match _____ St Andrew's School?

3. Everyone is going to the match _____ Peter — he has a cold.

4. Ken passed round his bag _____ sweets.

5. The plane is flying _____ a height _____ 10,000 metres.

6. Plants will die _____ water.

7. Is there anything good _____ the radio?

8. The play was written _____ an Australian writer.

9. Why don't you do something sensible _____ crying?

10. A giraffe is an animal _____ a very long neck.

11. Most children start school _____ the age _____ five.

12. The school timetable is now done _____ the computer.

13. Mum was digging the flower bed _____ a spade.

14. Our neighbours are away _____ holiday.

15. That looks _____ salt, not sugar.

28 Prepositions (3)

Adjectives, Nouns, Verbs used with Prepositions

- Some adjectives, nouns and verbs are used with a particular preposition: I'm **afraid of** wasps. Is there a **cure for** this disease? **Think of** a number.

A Put in a preposition to fill the gaps:

1. What was the answer ___*to*___ the puzzle?

2. I haven't paid _____ dinner yet.

3. I'm no good _____ dancing.

4. I'm still fond _____ my teddy bear.

5. Mum's looking _____ her spectacles.

6. What's wrong _____ my computer today?

7. Anna's eyes were full _____ tears.

8. Is there a good reason _____ all this noise?

9. Smoking causes damage _____ your lungs and heart.

10. I'm not used _____ large meals.

11. Are you interested _____ travel books?

12. Are you really listening _____ that radio programme?

13. Do you agree _____ me?

14. I can't help feeling sorry _____ the Ugly Sisters.

15. Your apartment is quite different _____ ours.

16. I don't believe _____ ghosts.

B Choose a preposition from the first box and form a verbal noun ending in **-ing** from a verb in the second box. Your will have to use some prepositions twice or more.

at	in	of	on

calculate	dance	drive	~~find~~	fish
get	read	sit	thank	win

1. The town's full; there's no possibility ___of finding___ a room for the night.

2. I'm not keen _____ and I don't like fish anyway.

3 Are you interested _____ as well as gymnastics?

4. I'd like to take this opportunity _____ my parents and friends for their generosity.

5. Grandad is 85, but he still insists _____ himself around the town.

6. Small babies are not capable _____ up by themselves.

7. There are several different ways _____ the total.

8. Many congratulations _____ the essay competition.

9. Why don't you buy her a book? She's very fond

_____ .

10. Mary is very clever _____ what she wants.

Prepositions left at the End (1)

- Prepositions often get left at the end of a sentence or phrase, for example when you use a **to**-infinitive or **for** + **-ing** to describe the purpose or use of something:

Here's a diagram **to look at**.

A chair is a piece of furniture **for sitting on**.

C Choose a verb from the first box to complete the **to**-infinitives or to form **-ing** nouns, and add a preposition from the second box. You will have to use some prepositions several times:

| hang | look | park | put | rely |
| rest | row | sit | talk | ~~wipe~~ |

| at | for | in | into | on |
| to | with | | | |

1. Have you a cloth to ___wipe___ the table ___with___ ?

2. Rocks aren't really very comfortable for _____ _____ .

3. You will need some oars to _____ the boat _____ .

4. I didn't find anybody to _____ _____ at the party.

5. What a boring magazine! There aren't any pictures to _____ _____ .

6. A footstool is a piece of furniture for _____ your feet _____ .

7. We all need a good friend to _____ _____ .

8. I'm looking for a space to _____ the car _____ .

9. Is there a strong plastic bag for _____ the rubbish _____ ?

10. There are some hooks over there for _____ your coats _____ .

D 1 Turn these sentences into the passive:

1. People are always shouting at me.
    I'm always being shouted at.

2. They are looking into the possibility.
    _____

3. They argued about the problem for hours.
    _____

4. They have checked through the figures.
    _____

D 2 Here are some answers. Make them questions that begin with who or what, leaving the preposition at the end.

1. Who is Jim talking to?
    Jim's talking to Sally.

2. _____
    Dad's angry about the mistake in the bill.

3. _____
    Bob's listening to a concert.

4. _____
    Mary danced with Peter.

D 3 Add the conclusion:

1. Joe is hunting for a pen. The pen is on the floor.
    The pen that Joe is hunting for is on the floor.

2. Dad is speaking to a man. The man is the manager.
    _____

3. We are going to look at an apartment. The apartment is in Bread Street.
    _____

4. I bumped into an old friend today. The old friend was on holiday here.
    _____

Prepositions left at the End (2)

There are three other important ways in which prepositions get left at the end of a sentence or clause when a verb is used with a preposition:

- Passives: if an active verb is used with a preposition, for example, People are staring at you, the passive form leaves the preposition at the end: You are being **stared at**.

- **Wh**-questions where the object is the **wh**-word: **What** are you **talking about**?

- Relative clauses: Here's **the book that** I was **looking for**.

29 PHRASAL VERBS (1)

- Phrasal verbs are verbs like **blow up**, or **switch on** or **laugh at**, that consist of a verb + an adverb or a preposition. The adverb or preposition is called a **particle**. The particle gives the verb a special meaning.

- Phrasal verbs, like ordinary verbs, can be **intransitive** (with no object) or **transitive** (with an object).

Intransitive Phrasal Verbs

- An intransitive verb + adverb makes an **intransitive phrasal verb**. It has no object.

A Add an adverb from the first box to turn the verbs into phrasal verbs (you'll have to use some of the adverbs several times). Then choose the right meaning from the second box.

along	down	in	off	out	up

to be friendly with somebody	to be not working
~~to be quick~~	to become an adult
to do things to make people notice you	to notice danger and take care
to leave the runway	to stop talking
to stop trying	to take part

1. We've no time to lose. **Hurry** ___up___ !   ___= to be quick___

2. Phone the garage. The car has **broken**

   _____ .   _____

3. What do you want to be when you **grow**

   _____ ?   _____

4. We're going to play football. Would you like

   to **join** _____ ?   _____

5. Are all the passengers aboard? The plane is

   ready to **take** _____ .   _____

6. **Watch** _____ ! There's a car coming! _____

7. Do **shut** _____ ! I'm trying to work. _____

8. We like each other — we **get** _____ OK. _____

9. We know you're a clever girl — there's no
   need to **show** _____ . _____

10. I don't know the answer to the riddle. I **give**

    _____ . _____

B Choose an adverb from the first box to
complete the phrasal verb. Then put brackets
round the object. Then choose the right
meaning from the second box.

| down | off | out | up |

to cancel	to collect	to confuse
to destroy by fire	to explode	to extinguish
to invent	to rear	to remove
to stop an electrical thing working		

1. I'll come and **pick** (you) ___up___ at the airport. ___= collect___

2. The weather was so bad that we had to **call**

   _____ the match. _____

3. People are always **mixing** the twins _____ . _____

4. The firemen managed to **put** _____ the fire. _____

5. For homework we all have to **make** _____
   a story. _____

6. Terrorists tried to **blow** _____ the tower. _____

7. Remember to **turn** the television _____ . _____

8. **Take** _____ your coat if you're too hot. _____

115

9. She has **brought** _____ three children on her own.   _____

10. A gang **burnt** the shop _____ a few years ago.   _____

Intransitive Verb + Preposition

■ Prepositions have objects, so an intransitive verb + preposition makes a **transitive phrasal verb**.

C Choose a preposition from the first box to complete the phrasal verb. Then put brackets round the object. Then choose the right meaning from the second box.

after	at	for	into	off	to	with

---

to accept an opportunity eagerly

to be amused by something

to be possessed by somebody

to be transformed

~~to force an entry~~

to have the same opinion

to leave a vehicle

to point a weapon at something

to take care of somebody

to try to find

---

1. Thieves **broke** _into_ (the shop) last night.   = to force an entry

2. Mum doesn't always **agree** _____ Dad.   _____

3. I'm **looking** _____ my schoolbag.   _____

4. Suddenly the witch **changed** _____ a beetle.   _____

5. Everybody **laughed** _____ Joe's joke.   _____

6. **Aim** carefully _____ the target.   _____

7. Ask the driver to tell you when to **get** _____ the bus.   _____

8. Those jeans **belong** _____ me.   _____

116

9. Nurses **look** _____ patients in a hospital. _____

10. Most of us would **jump** _____ the chance! _____

D The meanings are given to you. Find the adverb + preposition to complete the phrasal verb (you'll have to use some sets more than once). Then put brackets round the object:

Intransitive Verb + Adverb + Preposition

■ A phrasal verb that consists of a verb + adverb + preposition is a **transitive phrasal verb** because the preposition has an object.

| away from | down on | in for | off with |
| out in | out of | up for | up with |

1. Harry's always trying to **get** _____out of_____ (unpleasant tasks). (= to avoid doing something)

2. Somebody's **gone** _____ my calculator. (= to steal)

3. They like **going** _____ competitions. (= to enter a contest)

4. Don't walk so fast — I can't **keep** _____ you! (= to move at the same speed as somebody)

5. It's no good **running** _____ your problems. (= to try to escape)

6. I must go to the shop — we've **run** _____ food. (= to have no more of something)

7. The older pupils sometimes **look** _____ the younger ones. (= to treat somebody as less important than you)

8. I don't know how the British **put** _____ the cold! (= to bear something)

9. My elder brother always **stands** _____ me. (= to support somebody)

10. Some illnesses make you **come** _____ red spots. (= to be covered with a rash)

30 PHRASAL VERBS (2)

A Write out the particles and say whether they are adverbs or prepositions:

1. Miss Lee went over the explanation again.

   over – preposition

2. Keep away from the fire.

   away – adverb, from – preposition

3. Helen loves dressing up.

4. Read through the questions carefully.

5. Why don't you come round this evening?

6. The accident held the traffic up.

7. All these problems get you down.

8. Jim got into difficulties while swimming.

9. I must get down to work.

10. Let's get together sometime.

- If the particle is a preposition, the object comes after the preposition: I'll go through **the details** again.

- If the particle is an adverb, the object can usually come either between the verb and adverb or after the adverb:

   Put **the radio** on.

   Put on **the radio**.

   But if the object is a pronoun, it always comes between the verb and adverb:

   Put **it** on.

B Write the complete sentence, putting in the objects:

1. I don't let them push around (**me**)

   I don't let them push me around.

2. The curtains go with but the cushions don't go with (**the carpet, it**)

   _____

3. The soldiers laid explosives under the bridge and blew up (**it**)

   _____

4. I want to finish off before I go to bed (**my essay**)

   _____

5. You can always depend on to help (**her**)

   _____

6. They made some bad mistakes and tried to cover up (**them**)

   _____

7. They are threatening to close down next year (**the school**)

   _____

8. Miss Lee handed out at nine-thirty (**the exam papers**)

_____

9. Pick up and put away (**all these toys, them**)

_____

10. Hang up before somebody trips over (**your coat, it**)

_____

Making Phrasal Verbs Passive

■ When a phrasal verb is made passive, its object becomes its subject and the particle (preposition or adverb) follows the passive verb:

A neighbour is **looking after** the children. The children **are being looked after** by a neighbour.

They have **filled** the hole **in** again. The hole **has been filled in** again.

C Make these sentences passive:

1. Thieves often break into these apartments.

   These apartments are often broken into by thieves.

2. The head teacher sent round a notice.

   _____

3. The post office mixed their addresses up.

   _____

4. The other children sometimes laughed at Harry.

   _____

5. Dad had already turned the electricity off.

   _____

6. Somebody has crossed my name out.

   _____

7. A gang of bullies beat him up last night.

   _____

8. Jill left these dishes behind.

   _____

9. Some friends are caring for the baby.

   _____

10. The rest of the group soon caught me up.

    _____

D 1   Join the two sentences using **that**:

1.   We have a lot of work. We must get through it.

   We have a lot of work that we must get through.

2.   Here are some dry clothes. You can change into them.

   _____

3.   Have you a question? Would you like to bring it up?

   _____

4.   There's still a problem. We must deal with it.

   _____

5.   We all need goals. We can aim for them.

   _____

D 2   Join the two sentences using a **to**-infinitive:

6.   Here are some points. We can think over them.

   Here are some points to think over.

7.   Here's a raincoat. You can put it on.

   _____

8.   These are the right choices. We should go for them.

   _____

9.   I'm giving you an application form .You should fill it in.

   _____

10.   I have some more ideas. I can come back to them later.

   _____

CO-ORDINATING CONJUNCTIONS: AND, BUT, OR, SO

Joining Words and Phrases

- Use **and** to join similar things or ideas: Harry is often lazy **and** careless.

- Use **but** to join contrasting or different things or ideas: The message was short **but** helpful.

- Use **or** for a choice: You may have French fries **or** boiled potatoes.

- Use **or** instead of **and** with **not** and other negatives: I don't want French fries **or** boiled potatoes.

A Put in one of the conjunctions **and, but, or**:

1. Miss Lee is kind _____*but*_____ quite firm with her pupils.

2. The sea looked calm _____ flat.

3. In England we visited a lot of castles _____ palaces.

4. We didn't see many factories _____ offices.

5. Would you like an ice cream _____ an ice lolly?

6. George works fast _____ very accurately.

7. Is this lift going up _____ down?

8. The game was very strenuous _____ good fun.

9. I'm making a cake _____ sandwiches for tea.

10. I'm not sure whether to go right _____ left.

11. The dancer was rather fat _____ quite graceful.

12. What does he look like? Is he dark _____ fair?

B Write these examples out adding commas and **and** or **or**:

1. I need to buy some apples cheese milk tea coffee eggs.

   I need to buy some apples, cheese, milk, tea, coffee

   and eggs.

2. We don't need any carrots potatoes onions cooking oil noodles.

   _____

3. This morning I have maths English music history computer studies.

   _____

4. Shall we watch television go for a walk play football?

   _____

5. Find a large sheet of paper some coloured pens a pair of scissors.

   _____

6. I must finish my homework call Mary mend my bicycle write to Granny.

   _____

7. I don't know whether to go swimming sort out my photographs tidy my bedroom.

   _____

8. Pollution is a danger to wildlife rivers and lakes plants the atmosphere.

   _____

9. Is a spider an insect an animal what?

   _____

C Choose a sentence from the box to match one of the sentences below, and join them with **and, but, or** or **so**:

> ~~You didn't come.~~
>
> Shall I come to yours?
>
> The others are watching him.
>
> She wasn't at home.
>
> Put them in the fridge.
>
> Hold hands.
>
> I don't know how to do it.
>
> You may not smoke on this aircraft.
>
> Will Robert beat him?
>
> We decided to cancel the barbecue.

1. I waited for you at the corner.

   I waited for you at the corner but you didn't come.

2. Would you like to come to my house?

3. Jim is performing some acrobatics.

4. I called Granny.

5. Take these sausages.

6. I want to copy this material into another file.

7. You may unfasten your seatbelts now.

8. Find a partner.

9. Will Peter win?

_____

10. It was raining hard.

_____

D Change these **if-**sentences into **or-**sentences:

1. If you don't give back my doll I'll scream.

   Give back my doll or I'll scream.
   _____

2. If you don't hurry up you'll miss your bus.

   _____

3. If you don't stop pulling my hair I'll tell Mum.

   _____

4. If you don't do some work you'll fail your exams.

   _____

5. If you don't hold on to the rail you'll slip.

   _____

6. If you don't move your bicycle somebody will trip over it.

   _____

7. If you don't have your soup now it'll get cold.

   _____

8. If you don't tell me the truth you'll get no pocket money.

   _____

9. If you don't lend me your handphone I won't help you.

   _____

10. If you don't act now you'll miss your chance.

    _____

32 CONJUNCTIONS AND CLAUSES (1)

Time Clauses

- You can put time clauses and many other kinds of subordinate clause before or after the main clause: She screamed **when she saw the ghost**. **When she saw the ghost**, she screamed.

- You can put a comma after the subordinate clause if it comes first: **When the ghost spoke**, she fainted.

A Choose time clauses from column 1 to go **before** five of the main clauses below, and choose time clauses from column 2 to go **after** the other five main clauses.

Write out the whole sentence with a capital letter and a full stop, and underline the conjunction:

1	2
After I've eaten my breakfast	as we said goodbye
As soon as Peter got home	~~since I last saw him~~
When the sun rose	till the bus comes
When you were in India	when you see her
While the car park is being altered	while they washed and changed

1. he's grown a beard

   He's grown a beard <u>since</u> I last saw him

2. give Jane this message

3. we felt very sad

4. I'm ready to face the day.

5. I cooked a meal for the guests

6. he fed his pet rabbit

126

7. the birds began to sing

   _____

8. we'll have to park in the street

   _____

9. did you see the Taj Mahal?

   _____

10. wait quietly at the bus stop

   _____

B Complete the sentences using the verbs in the box in the right form:

apply	arrive	come	contact	do
go	leave	make	start	tell

Time Conjunctions + Simple Present

■ The time conjunctions **when, before, till, as soon as, while** are used with the simple present when the main clause contains a future form of the verb:

I'**ll wait** here till you **come**.

When I **visit** Italy, I'**m going to stay** in Rome.

1. Dad is going to wait in the car while Mum _____*does*_____ the shopping.

2. As soon as I get my exam results, I __'ll apply__ for a university.

3. She says she'll find a job in London when she

   _____ to Britain.

4. Will you keep a place in the queue for him till he

   _____ back?

5. I'll check that all the windows are closed before I

   _____ the apartment.

6. When I'm in your town next month, I _____ you.

7. Helen is going to call us as soon as she _____ at the airport.

8. He'll think very carefully before he _____ a decision.

9. You'll feel better as soon as you _____ the course of pills.

10. Before I describe the play, I _____ you about the author.

If -Clauses (1)

- The conjunctions **if** and **as long as** are used with a simple present when the main clause has a future form of the verb:

  If I **see** Jean, I**'ll pass** on the message to her.

  He**'s going to apply** for Singapore University if he **passes** all his exams.

  She**'ll do** fine as long as she **keeps** calm.

- **Unless** means the same as **if not**: We'll come tomorrow **unless** there's a change of plan.

C **Complete the sentences using the verbs in the box in the right form:**

apply	be	buy	come	eat
do	get	rain	remember	work

1. I _'ll eat_____ your ice cream if you don't want it.

2. We shall be able to keep in contact with him as long as

   he _____ to use his handphone.

3. If he _____ for a visa, he'll be able to stay in Taiwan for some time.

4. She _____ into trouble if she doesn't watch out.

5. You'll see the sea if you _____ to this window.

6. If Joe _____ well in his exams, he'll train as a doctor.

7. If there _____ a ring round the moon, it's likely to rain.

8. Unless he _____ harder, he won't get good grades.

9. I'll buy the drink if you _____ the sandwiches.

10. The barbecue will go ahead unless it _____ heavily.

D **Complete the sentences using a verb from the box in the right form:**

be	care	come	concentrate	fall
find	forget	get	have	sneeze

1. You would read more fluently if you _concentrated_ more.

2. If I __hadn't__ ~~not~~ __fallen__ over, I might have won the race.

3. I wouldn't have found you if you _____ not _____ .

4. You would look better if you _____ your hair cut.

5. I would buy an island if I _____ the money.

6. We would be millionaires if we _____ that treasure.

7. We could do a parachute jump if we _____ brave enough.

8. There wouldn't have been a problem if you _____ not _____ your passport.

9. You could have been injured if a train _____ along.

10. I wouldn't make a fuss if I _____ not _____ about you.

If -Clauses (2)

■ *When the main clause has* **would** *or* **might** *or* **could,** *the* **if**-*clause has a form of the verb that is the same as the simple past: You* **might** *win if you* **trained** *properly.*

■ *When the main clause has* **might have** *or* **would have** *or* **could have,** *the* **if**-*clause has the past perfect: You* **might have** *won if you* **had trained** *properly.*

33 CONJUNCTIONS AND CLAUSES (2): REASON, PURPOSE, RESULT, CONCESSION

Reason: Because, As, Since, In Case

■ You use the conjunctions **because**, **as**, **since** and **in case** to give the reason for saying something or to say why something happens.

A Choose a clause from the box to complete the sentences:

> he isn't old enough
>
> I had a headache
>
> it's the last day of term
>
> take a book to read
>
> we'll take the tram
>
> ~~we're not certain of the route~~
>
> you may hurt somebody's feelings
>
> you tell me the answer then
>
> you're the eldest
>
> you weren't at the cafe

1. Since ___we're not certain of the route___ , we'd better start early.

2. I went to bed without any dinner because _____ .

3. As _____ , you can be in charge of the others.

4. He can't take his driving test because _____ .

5. _____ in case you get bored.

6. Since _____ , I just went home again.

7. _____ because it's so difficult to find a parking space in town.

8. Sometimes you daren't tell the truth because

_____ .

9. As _____ , you can read your comics in class.

10. _____ , since you're so clever.

B Put in **in order that, so that, in order to** or **so as to**:

1. I went to bed early _____*so as to*_____ (or _____*in order to*_____) be able to catch the train next morning.

2. Speak clearly _____ the audience can hear you.

3. We'll have to wait some hours _____ the paint has time to dry.

4. I sometimes write telephone numbers on my hand

_____ remind myself of them.

5. Susie always folds her clothes neatly

_____ they don't crease.

6. You should eat this fruit soon _____ it doesn't go bad.

7. Eat plenty of fresh fruit _____ stay strong and healthy.

8. You can record the songs on tape _____ remember them better.

9. Stand in a line _____ I can count you.

10. Please move up _____ make more room.

- You use **so** before an adjective or adverb: He's **so stingy** that he won't even buy a newspaper. I clapped **so hard** that my hands hurt.

- You use **such a** before a noun (or **such** before an uncountable or plural noun), even if the noun has an adjective before it: I had **such a headache** that I fainted. I had **such a bad headache** that I fainted. We had **such wonderful weather** that we all got a nice tan.

C Put in **such a, such** or **so**:

1. She got _____such a_____ nasty shock that she had to sit down for a minute.

2. The children were _____ excited that they couldn't sleep.

3. He did _____ badly in the exam that he had to sit it again.

4. It was _____ lovely day that we stayed on the beach longer than we meant to.

5. We'd had _____ tiring journey that we had to rest for a day.

6. His hair was _____ long that people thought he was a girl.

7. There was _____ noise that I couldn't hear what they were saying.

8. We had _____ comfortable beds that we slept till 10 o'clock.

9. We slept _____ soundly that we didn't hear the alarm clock.

10. They bought _____ expensive material that they had no money left for lunch.

D Choose a clause from the box to complete the sentences:

> everybody's welcome to join the course
> he's still in good health
> I had to sing a solo in the concert
> she's good at drawing horses
> she's only ten herself
> Mum usually laughs
> the grammar is difficult
> we started the second book
> you aren't successful
> you think it sounds silly

1. I enjoy learning English even though _____

   _____ .

2. Although I'm no good at singing _____ ,

   _____ .

3. It's worth taking part in the competition even if

   _____ .

4. Although _____ ,
   he's decided to retire from work.

5. Say the words aloud to yourself even if

   _____ .

6. _____ , even though
   we hadn't quite finished the first one.

7. _____ , even if they
   know nothing about computers.

8. Anna is good at looking after the other children although

   _____ .

9. Although _____ ,
   she can't draw people.

10. _____ , even though
    she doesn't approve of my jokes.

34 RELATIVE CLAUSES: WHO, WHOM, WHICH, THAT

■ It will help you to look again at Unit 5.

A Choose a set of words from the box that describes the person, animal or thing below, and use **who** or **which** to complete the description:

fits showers and mends pipes	has prickles to protect it
helps you do sums	is man-made
measures temperature	performs operations
plays the flute	~~preys on small animals~~
supports your head	watch an event

1. An eagle is a bird

   which preys on small animals.

2. A surgeon is a doctor

   _____

3. A plumber is a person

   _____

4. A calculator is a gadget

   _____

5. A pillow is a kind of cushion

   _____

6. A hedgehog is an animal

   _____

7. A flautist is a musician

   _____

8. A thermometer is an instrument

   _____

9. Plastic is a substance

_____

10. Spectators are people

_____

B Join these two pieces of information together using a relative clause. Use the relative pronouns **who** (or **that**) or **which** (or **that**) if the relative pronoun is the subject of the relative clause, but leave it out if it is the object of the relative clause:

Omitting Relative Pronouns

■ You need the relative pronoun **who, which** or **that** if it is the **subject** of the relative clause: The girl **who** (or **that**) **telephoned** left a message for you.

■ You can leave out the relative pronoun if it is the object of the relative clause, or the object of a preposition in the relative clause:

The girl ~~that (or who or whom)~~ you telephoned called back again.

The film ~~that (or which)~~ I was telling you about is on television tonight.

1. The plane was waiting on the runway. It has now taken off.

    The plane that (or which) was waiting on the runway has

    now taken off.

2. We hired a car. It was bright blue.

    The car we hired was bright blue.

3. A doctor treated my injury. He was from Thailand.

    _____

4. Anna lent me an umbrella. It's hanging over there.

    _____

5. A strange noise woke us in the night. It was the foghorn.

    _____

6. I was trying to contact a friend. He was away on holiday.

    _____

7. We made friends with some passengers. They were Scottish.

    _____

8. Jane bought a hair-dryer. It was faulty.

    _____

9. You're sitting in an armchair. It was my mother's.

_____

10. A man opened the door. He was tall and thin.

_____

Using Where as a Relative Pronoun

■ You can use **where** like a relative pronoun when you are referring to a place.

For example, instead of saying: The apartment **I'm staying in** belongs to a friend,

you can say: The apartment **where I'm staying** belongs to a friend.

C 1 Change these examples to the where kind of relative clause:

1. The hospital Granny was taken to is quite nearby.
   The hospital where Granny was taken is quite nearby.

2. The shop I bought your present in is closing down.

_____

3. The youth hostel they stayed at was very comfortable.

_____

4. The hall we're performing our concert in holds 1000 people.

_____

5. The shelf the dictionary sits on is over there.

_____

C 2 Change these examples to the kind of relative clause with a preposition at the end, using the preposition in brackets.

1. The garage where our car was repaired wasn't too far away. (**at**)
   The garage our car was repaired at wasn't too far away.

2. The bench where I was sitting was not very steady. (**on**)

_____

3. The park where the children play has swings and a climbing frame. (**in**)

_____

4. The hotel where they stayed had a swimming pool. (**at**)

_____

5. The book where I found the map is kept in the car. (**in**)

_____

D Join the two pieces of information together, using **who**, **whom**, **which** or **where**. You can use **who** or **whom** if it is the object.

1. I met Charles. I didn't recognize him at first.

   I met Charles, whom (or who) I didn't recognize at first.

2. We are going to visit Taiwan. I was born there.

   We are going to visit Taiwan, where I was born.

3. The door was opened by Harry. He was wearing his gym clothes.

   _____

4. We went to look for our car. We had parked it in a side street.

   _____

5. Jennifer is going to marry Steven. She met him at a dance.

   _____

6. We visited the Tower of London. It stands beside the River Thames.

   _____

7. I waited in the Café Politique. I'd arranged to meet Sue there.

   _____

8. I've just been to the dentist. She said my teeth were in perfect condition.

   _____

9. We all met outside the hotel. The bus was standing there ready for us.

   _____

10. I had a long conversation with Angela. I hadn't seen her for three years.

    _____

Relative Clauses that add information

■ You can use relative clauses beginning with **who, whom, which** and **where** to add a further piece of information about the person, thing or place you have just mentioned. You always put a comma before this kind of relative clause:

I phoned Maggie, **who had just woken up**.

We arrived in London, **where we stayed for five days**.

35 Noun Clauses: Reporting People's Speech and Thoughts

That

- You use the conjunction **that** after saying or thinking verbs, to report the words that people speak, or the thoughts they have: *Charlie said* **that** *the plane was late. I thought* **that** *you were away on holiday.*

- The part of the sentence containing the speaker's words or the thinker's thoughts is called a **noun clause**. The conjunction **that** is often left out: *Charlie said* **the plane was late.** *I thought* **you were away on holiday**.

A Use the conjunction **that** and choose a clause from the box, to fill the gap:

> ~~a spider was an insect~~
> he's moving house soon.
> I left my calculator in my desk
> I shouldn't eat so much
> Mum could use the computer
> she wants to be a musician
> she was the right person for the job
> the earthquake was only a small one
> the flight was on time
> the match was cancelled

1. I thought _____ that a spider was an insect _____ , but I was wrong.

2. Jean is good at the violin and says _____ _____ .

3. I'm sure _____ , but I can't find it now.

4. Ken lives next door to me but he tells me _____ .

5. I know _____ but I get so hungry.

6. It was announced at Assembly today ____ _ ____ _____ .

7. I'm certain _____ but she's scared to try.

8. We believe _____ but we're waiting for more news.

9. Mum convinced the manager _____

    _____ .

10. We were informed at the airport enquiry desk

    _____ .

B **Write out the whole group of words that belong to the noun clause:**

1. When I heard the amazing news I thought I was going to faint.

    I **was going to faint** _____

2. They told us the apartment would be available in two weeks' time.

    _____

3. He knows he can't win but he's keen to try.

    _____

4. Do you really believe the plan will succeed?

    _____

5. I was told you were looking for me.

    _____

6. I hadn't realized you painted that picture yourself.

    _____

7. It is thought he just died in his sleep.

    _____

8. I don't think it's right to kill insects, but others may disagree.

    _____

9. I'm sure you don't want to listen to all this nonsense.

    _____

10. Did you say you were going out tonight?

    _____

Identifying Noun Clauses

■ The conjunction **that** is often left out between the saying or thinking verb and the noun clause: I realised ~~that~~ I **needed my passport for the journey**.

Asking and Wondering: If and Whether

■ You use the conjunctions **if** and **whether** after verbs of asking, finding out, wondering or not knowing, to report questions that people ask others or ask themselves:

George asked me **if** (or **whether**) I'd finished my essay.

I wonder **whether** (or **if**) Sarah got the job.

Mike isn't sure **if** (or **whether**) he can come.

C Use **if** or **whether** and choose a clause from the box to fill the gap:

> he can drive you to your dancing class
>
> he'll remember to bring his kit
>
> it's going to clear up
>
> ~~she would like to dance with him~~
>
> she's any good at acting
>
> she's better yet
>
> the others are awake yet
>
> the train from Leeds had arrived
>
> the washing machine had finished
>
> we'd brought our atlases to school

1. John asked Susan _if (or whether) she would like to_ _dance with him_ .

2. I went into the kitchen to find out _____ _____ .

3. Sally has been ill — I don't know _____ .

4. Miss Lee asked us _____ .

5. It's still raining — I doubt _____ _____ .

6. It's time to get up — I'll see _____ _____ .

7. Ask Dad _____ .

8. At the station we enquired _____ _____ .

9. Carol's keen to be in the play, but I wonder _____ _____ .

10. I'll remind Dave about the match, because I'm not sure _____ .

D Put in one of the **wh**-question words:

how	what	when	where
which	who	whom	why

1. Can you say ___why___ the temperature drops at night?

2. Let me know _____ you are arriving.

3. We tried to find out _____ Dave was taking to the dance.

4. Do you know _____ you want to be when you grow up?

5. Show me _____ you attached that file to your e-mail.

6. Miss Lee explained _____ parallel lines get closer together in the distance.

7. Dad asked us _____ of the four flavours of ice cream we'd prefer.

8. I've no idea _____ played that trick on you.

9. We enquired _____ the museum was.

10. We also wanted to know _____ time the museum opened.

Asking, Telling Wondering, and Explaining: What, Who, Whom, Which, Why, How, Where, When

- You can use all these **wh**- question words as conjunctions after verbs of asking, wondering, telling and explaining:

  Mum asked John **what** he wanted for dinner.

  I don't know **how** you got that idea.

  Tell me **why** you never turned up for the match.

- You can use **who** or **whom** when it is the object

36 PHRASES

- A **noun phrase** is a group of words that plays the part of a **noun** in a sentence. So it can be the subject or object of a verb, or the object of a preposition:

  The trading settlement of Singapore was founded in 1819.

  Harry beats **most of his friends** at chess.

  I threw **the rubbish** into **the wastepaper basket**.

- A noun phrase can also be used to explain a noun, or a proper noun:

  Mum was talking to Mrs Chen, **our next-door neighbour**.

- A **phrase** is a group of words that does a grammatical job, for example as a noun, adjective or adverb.

A Underline the noun phrases in these sentences. There may be more than one in some sentences:

1. Put <u>your maths textbooks</u> away, please.

2. I'm giving you some grammar exercises for your English homework.

3. We're performing *Macbeth*, one of Shakespeare's plays.

4. I found some pretty shells on the beach and added them to my large collection.

5. Mary, my cousin from London, is visiting us soon.

6. Lucy examined the curious purple envelope carefully before opening it.

7. Look at these splendid red apples that I bought at the local supermarket.

8. Joe gave his last coin to a ragged child.

9. Yesterday I met Mark, an old friend of mine.

10. There are three good reasons why I can't play in Saturday's match.

■ An **adverbial phrase** plays the part of an **adverb** and says something about the action of the verb, for example, its place or time or manner. Adverbial phrases may start with a preposition, or they may contain adverbs:

Dad laid his newspaper **on the table**.

She only works **in the mornings**.

Leaves were whirling **here and there**.

You have done the job **very thoroughly**.

■ Sentence adverbs, which you use to add your own comments on a situation, are often in the form of adverbial phrases:

On the whole, I'd rather not be an actor.

By the way, there's no milk left.

B Underline the adverbial phrases in these sentences:

1. In my opinion, she behaved extremely sensibly.

2. For once the train arrived on time.

3. We shall be leaving at four o'clock.

4. Dad explained the process in great detail.

5. Come and sit beside me.

6. Watch once again, a bit more carefully.

7. We played tennis until half past six.

8. He walks very slowly with a stick.

9. We're going abroad during the vacation.

10. At least I played my part pretty well in the play.

- An **adjectival phrase**, like an **adjective**, describes a noun.

- Adjectival phrases can begin with prepositions and come after the noun they describe: Who is that girl **with blonde hair**? The fruit **on this tree** is even sweeter.

- Adjectival phrases can also begin with participles: The parcel **sitting on the table** is for you. He showed us a page **torn out of a magazine**.

C Underline the adjectival phrases in these sentences:

1. The books <u>on this shelf</u> still need to be dusted.

2. Ask the lady in the blue uniform.

3. The label attached to the chicken gives cooking instructions.

4. Who sits at the desk in the corner?

5. Dad was talking to a man with a beard.

6. They collect money for people without homes.

7. The path through the park was muddy.

8. The pictures on the wall were all drawn by the children.

9. The man standing in front of me suddenly stepped backwards.

10. Is this the bus for Melaka?

Adjectival Phrases before the Noun

■ When you put an adjectival phrase before a noun, you sometimes need hyphens to join up the words, to make it easier for people to read:

These children are ten years old. They're **ten-year-old** children.

The name Barbara has three syllables. It's a **three-syllable** name.

This banknote is worth five dollars. It's a **five-dollar** banknote.

That word sounds strange. It's a **strange-sounding** word.

D Use the words after the verb to form an adjectival phrase before the noun:

1. The timetable is out of date. It's an ___out-of-date___ timetable.

2. The baby is two months old. She's a _____ baby.

3. Our family has two cars. We're a _____ family.

4. We were delayed for two hours. We had a _____ delay.

5. The booklet has eight pages. It's an _____ booklet.

6. Their methods are up to date. They use _____ methods.

7. That cheese smells horrible. It's _____ cheese.

8. The house was built in the eighteenth century. It is an _____ house.

9. That building looks very odd. It's a very _____ building.

10. The journey lasted three days. It was a _____ journey.

37 NEGATIVE SENTENCES

> ### Negative Sentences formed with Not
>
> - If the verb in a sentence consists of a helping verb such as **can, may, will, must** + a main verb such as **sing, eat, run, play,** the word **not** is placed immediately after the helping verb: You **must not stay**. The parcel **may not arrive** today.
>
> - If there is more than one helping verb, **not** is placed after the **first** one: She **might not be coming** to the party. You **should not have done** that.
>
> - The shortened form of **not** is **-n't**. **-n't** is always attached to the verb it follows: I **don't know** what to do. She **isn't coming**. You **couldn't have prevented** the accident.
>
> - When **can** is followed by **not**, the two words are written as one single word: I **cannot** understand a word she says.
>
> Remember that you can shorten **will not** to **won't**, **cannot** to **can't**, **shall not** to **shan't**.

A Make the following sentences negative by putting in **not** or **-n't** in the correct position:

1. I **might come** back next year. (**not**)

   I might not come back next year.

2. We **are going** to get the job finished by next week. (**-n't**)

   We aren't going to get the job finished by next week.

3. We **may have finished** the job by next week. (**not**)

   _____

4. I **would like** to live in Africa. (**-n't**)

   _____

5. I **can imagine** what she was thinking. (**not**)

   _____

6. Learning French at school **might have changed** my life. (**not**)

   _____

146

7. This is the kind of silly behaviour teachers **should ignore**. (**not**)

   _____

8. You **can park** your car over there. (**-n't**)

   _____

9. She said she **would be** here tomorrow. (**-n't**)

   _____

10. She **will come** back again. (**-n't**)

   _____

B Make the following sentences negative by putting in **not** and the correct form of the helping verb **do**. The form of the main verb may also have to be changed:

1. My little sisters **like** ice-cream. (**-n't**)

   My little sisters don't like ice cream.

2. We **enjoyed** the concert. (**not**)

   We did not enjoy the concert.

3. He **eats** a lot of fish (**-n't**)

   _____

4. I **understand** the question. (**-n't**)

   _____

5. The man **hesitated** for a second before jumping out of the plane. (**not**)

   _____

6. We **saw** Mary in town this morning. (**-n't**)

   _____

7. Who **wants** coffee? (**-n't**)

   _____

Negative Sentences formed with Not and Do

■ If there is no other helping verb in the sentence, then the helping verb **do** is used along with **not** or **-n't**:

I **understand** why she said that.
I **do not understand** why she said that.

My mother **gave** me the money.
My mother **didn't give** me the money.

Close that window.
Don't close that window.

8. The children **slept** all night. (**not**)

_____

9. They **managed** to pull the sheep out of the ditch. (**-n't**)

_____

10. I **knew** what to do. (**-n't**)

_____

11. The policeman **asked** for our names. (**-n't**)

_____

12. The boys **thought** they had enough money for the train fare home. (**not**)

_____

Negative Sentences formed with words such as No, None, Never, Nothing, Nobody

■ Some negative sentences are formed with negative words such as **no**, **none**, **never**, **nothing**, **nobody**, rather than with **not** or **-n't**.

C Choose a suitable negative word from the box and make the following sentences negative:

neither	never	no	nobody
none	no-one	nothing	nowhere

1. We **always** go to Australia for our summer holidays.

   We never go to Australia for our summer holidays.

2. We have **some** food left.

   _____

3. There is **somebody** in the garden.

   _____

4. There is **something** wrong with the car.

   _____

5. There is **someone** else I can ask for help.

   _____

6. 'How many sums did you get wrong?' '**A few.**'

    _____

7. **Many** of the passengers in the train were injured in the crash.

    _____

8. **Many** passengers were injured in the crash.

    _____

9. There were two men in the shop. **One** of them spoke English.

    _____

10. There were three men in the shop. **One** of them spoke English.

    _____

D Make the following sentences negative using the words in brackets, and making all other necessary changes:

1. I **always** go **somewhere** exciting for my summer holidays. (**never**)

    I never go anywhere exciting for my summer holidays.

2. She **has** forgotten the accident and you **should** forget it **too**. (**-n't**)

    She hasn't forgotten the accident and you shouldn't

    forget it either.

3. We **might** buy **some** more bread. (**not**)

    _____

4. My sister says she **always** meets **someone** interesting at her friend's parties. (**never**)

    _____

Other Changes that must be made in Negative Sentences

■ When a positive sentence is made negative by means of a negative word such as **not, never, no,** etc, there may be some other changes that need to be made to the sentence as well:

I can see **someone.**
I can**'t** see **anyone.**

We shall go **too.**
We shan**'t** go **either.**

Some of the guests have **already** arrived.
None of the guests have arrived **yet.**

5. She **may** have **something** important to tell you. (**not**)

_____

6. There **will** be **someone** to help you carry your bags. (**-n't**)

_____

7. There **might** be **something someone** could do to help them. (**not**)

_____

8. My sister **has** been invited to the party and I **have** been invited **too**. (**-n't**)

_____

9. She **drinks** tea and she **drinks** coffee **as well**. (**-n't**)

_____

10. **Some** voting stations are **already** open. (**no**)

_____

11. I **have already** had lunch. (**-n't**)

_____

12. **Some** of your friends have brought **some** food with them **too**. (**none**)

_____

38 QUESTIONS

- **Yes**-or-**no** questions are questions that expect a **yes** or a **no** as their answer:

  Are you coming with us? **Yes.**   *Can I go with you?* **No.**

  Is your father a teacher? **Yes.**   *Does he have a dog? (or: Has he got a dog?)* **No.**

- To form **yes**-or-**no** questions, you use the verbs **be, have,** or any of the other helping verbs such as **do** or **can** or **may**. The subject of the verb is placed immediately after the helping verb, or after the first helping verb if there is more than one:

  *Is **she** still here? Have **you** any explanation for the explosion? Will **it** rain again tomorrow? Will **it** be raining again tomorrow? Could **you** have done anything to help?*

A Change the following statements into **yes**-or-**no** questions:

1. Her brother speaks French and German.

   Does her brother speak French and German?

2. They will have finished the project by the end of next week.

   _____

3. We must leave at once.

   _____

4. He's coming round to see us tomorrow night.

   _____

5. She was very upset when she heard the news.

   _____

6. The boys want to come with us to the circus.

   _____

7. She was a close friend of the head teacher.

   _____

8. She said she was a close friend of the head teacher.

   _____

9. There's something wrong with my calculations.

_____

10. The children were singing as they walked through the woods.

_____

Not and -n't in Yes-or-No Questions

■ In negative **yes**-or-**no** questions formed with **-n't**, the **-n't** is attached to **be, have,** or the first helping verb in the sentence: Is**n't** she here yet? Could**n't** you come back some other time? Have**n't** you seen that film?

■ In negative **yes**-or-**no** questions formed with **not** or with other negative words such as **never**, the negative word follows the subject of the sentence: Is she **not** here yet? Could the electrician **not** come back some other time? Have you **never** seen that film?

B Make the following statements into negative **yes**-or-**no** questions using the negative word given in brackets:

1. That **was** a rather silly thing to do. (**-n't**)

   Wasn't that a rather silly thing to do?
   _____

2. They **would be** able to help you. (**not**)

   Would they not be able to help you?
   _____

3. They **would be** able to help you. (**-n't**)

   _____

4. It**'s** time the children were in bed. (**-n't**)

   _____

5. We **saw** that man on television last night. (**-n't**)

   _____

6. You **could have invited** them to the wedding. (**-n't**)

   _____

7. The boys **can stay** a little bit longer. (**not**)

_____

8. They**'ve been** to France. (**never**)

_____

9. Her parents **like** pop music. (**not**)

_____

10. The hedge **needs** cutting again. (**-n't**)

_____

Wh-Questions

- **Wh**-questions are questions formed with the words **who?**, **whom?**, **whose?**, **which?**, **what?**, **when?**, **where?**, **why?** and **how?** along with the verbs **be, have,** or any of the helping verbs.

- The question word stands at the beginning of the sentence: **Where** are you? **Who** did that? **Whose** handphone is this?

- If the question word is not the subject of the sentence (or part of the subject), the subject comes after the verb, or after the first verb if there is more than one: Where are **you**? What are **you** doing? Why should **I** have offered to help them?

- The rules for the position of negative words are the same as in **yes**-or-**no** questions: Why should**n't** I have offered to help them? Why should I **not** have offered to help them? Why am I **never** allowed to go to the shops on my own?

C Choose one of the question words in the box and fill in the gaps in the following questions:

how	what	when	~~where~~	which
who	whom	whose	why	

1. '____Where____ are you?' 'I'm over here.'

2. '_____ did you get here?' 'We came by train.'

3. '_____ happened?' 'A car broke down and blocked the road.'

4. '_____ did you get here?' 'About three o'clock.'

5. '_____ books are these?' 'Peter's, I think.'

6. '_____ should I send the letter to?' 'Send it to the manager.'

7. 'To _____ should I send the letter?' 'Send it to the manager.'

8. '_____ cake would you like?' 'That chocolate one.'

9. '_____ do I have to go to bed now?' 'Because it's your bed-time.'

10. 'To _____ do you owe your success?' 'A lot of hard work and a bit of luck.'

Idioms and Special Phrases using Wh-Question words

■ There are a number of idioms and special phrases in the form of **wh**-questions using **what** and **how**: **What**'s up? **What** is it like? **How** about a trip to the seaside? **What** about buying her a new handbag?

D Use a **wh**-question word to fill in the gaps in the following questions:

1. '____What____'s up? Why is Mary looking so upset?' 'She has just learnt that her father is very ill.'

2. 'I've just bought a new car.' 'Oh? _____'s it like?

3. 'I've no idea what to give my mother for her birthday.'

   '_____ about giving her some flowers or a pot plant?'

4. _____ do you do? My name is Peter Simpson.

5. '_____ time is it?' 'About half past six.'

6. '_____ is it like being the youngest dancer in the company?' 'Well, everyone is very kind to me.'

7. I really like that wallpaper. _____ about you?

8. _____'s the matter? Why are you crying?

9. _____ if no-one heard you calling for help? What would you do then?

10. 'I've just met our new neighbours.' 'Oh? _____ they like?'

39 REPORTED SPEECH

Direct and Indirect Speech

- **Direct speech** shows the exact words that a person has said or written or thought:

  '**There is a strange bird in the garden**,' said Helen.

  '**They're wrong**,' I thought.

- **Indirect speech** or **reported speech** gives the same information in the form of a noun clause reporting what was said or written or thought:

  Helen said **that there was a strange bird in the garden**.

  I thought **that they were wrong**.

- The conjunction **that** can be left out in reported speech or thought: I thought ~~that~~ they were wrong.

- When the saying or thinking verb is in the present tense, the tense of the verb in reported speech is the same as it would be in direct speech:

  I **think** they **are** wrong. (The exact words I am thinking are: 'They **are** wrong.')

  Mary **says** the boys **have**n't been seen. (The exact words Mary is saying are: 'The boys **have**n't been seen.')

- When the saying or thinking verb is in the past tense, verbs that were in the present tense in direct speech must become past tenses in reported speech, and verbs that were past tenses in direct speech must become past perfect in reported speech:

  I **thought** they **were** wrong. (The exact words I thought were: 'They **are** wrong.')

  Mary **said** the boys **had**n't been seen. (The exact words that Mary said are: 'The boys **have**n't been seen.')

A Choose the correct tense for the verb to fill the gaps:

1. 'The treatment is absolutely painless,' said the dentist.

   The dentist said that the treatment ____was____ absolutely painless.

2. I said, 'We're going the wrong way.'

   I said that we _____ going the wrong way.

3. 'We haven't seen John all day,' we said to the teacher.

   We told the teacher that we _____ seen John all day.

4. 'Mrs Lin is going to live with her sister in Taiwan,' said Mrs Chen.

    Mrs Chen said that Mrs Lin _____ going to live with her sister in Taiwan.

5. 'Banana trees aren't really trees,' said the teacher.

    The teacher told the class that banana trees _____ really trees.

6. 'Sheila's feeling fine after her operation,' says her mother.

    Sheila's mother says that Sheila _____ feeling fine after her operation.

7. 'The cows have eaten all the turnips,' complained the farmer.

    The farmer complained that the cows _____ eaten all the turnips.

8. 'I don't like coffee,' I said.

    I said that I _____ like coffee.

9. 'The train leaves in five minutes,' I told them.

    I told them that the train _____ in five minutes.

10. We've been waiting for more than an hour,' we said.

    We said that we _____ been waiting for more than half an hour.

Helping Verbs in Reported Speech

■ When the saying or thinking verb is in the past tense, helping verbs such as **can** and **may** must be changed to past-tense forms. **Can** must be changed to **could, will** and **shall** to **would**, and **may** to **might**:

I **will** go. I **thought** I **would** go.

The boys **can** go. Mary **said** the boys **could** go.

B Choose the correct form for the helping verb. Use short forms if short forms are used in the direct speech:

1. 'John will come again soon,' I assured them.

    I assured them that John _____*would*_____ come again soon.

2. I'll never speak to her again.

    I tell you I _____'ll_____ never speak to her again.

3. I'll never speak to her again,' I said.

    I said that I _____ never speak to her again.

156

4. I'll never get another chance,' she thought.

   She was sure that she _____ never get another chance.

5. 'We can't eat another thing,' we said.

   We said that we _____ eat another thing.

6. 'We shall certainly meet again somewhere,' I told her.

   I told her that we _____ certainly meet again somewhere.

7. 'I'm sorry we shan't be able to be at the party,' I said.

   I said that I _____ sorry we _____ be able to be at the party.

8. 'I hate potatoes,' I said

   I said that I _____ potatoes.

9. 'I can't see anything,' I told her.

   'll

   I told her that I _____ see anything.

10. 'We did try to help,' we said.

    We said that we _____ tried to help.

C Put in suitable forms for reported speech:

1. 'I went for a long walk yesterday,' said James.

   James said that ___*he had gone*___ for a long walk ___*the day before*___ .

2. 'I'm sick and tired of your laziness,' Sarah said to her brother.

   Sarah told her brother that _____ sick and tired of _____ laziness.

3. 'I'm surprised to see you here,' I said to her.

   I said that I _____ surprised to see _____ .

4. 'I don't like coffee,' said the girl.

   The girl said that _____ like coffee.

5. 'My sister is going to be a nurse,' Mary told her friend.

   Mary told her friend that _____ sister

   _____ going to be a nurse.

6. 'We saw a strange man outside the shop just before the robbery,' said the children.

   The children told the police that _____ a strange man outside the shop just before the robbery.

7. 'We taught English in Japan for a year,' the couple next door told me.

   The couple next door told me that _____ English in Japan for a year.

8. 'My leg hurts,' she complained.

   She complained that _____ leg _____ .

9. 'I shall be back,' said Arnie.

   Arnie said _____ be back.

10. 'I can't come tomorrow,' said Tom.

    Tom said that _____ come _____ .

- Questions in reported speech are called **indirect questions**.

- To make indirect questions from direct **yes**-or-**no** questions, you use **if** or **whether**:
  'Is everyone here?' asked Mary. Mary asked **if** (or **whether**) everyone was there.

- To make indirect **wh**-questions, you use the same **wh**-words as in the direct questions:
  '**Why** did you say that?' she asked. She asked **why** I had said that.

- In indirect questions the subject comes **before** the verb, not after it as in many direct questions. You do not use **do** as a helping verb to form indirect questions:
  'Do you take sugar?' Henry asked her. Henry asked her if **she took** sugar.
  'What do you think?' Harry asked her. Harry asked her what **she thought**.

- Indirect **wh**-questions sometimes use a **to**-infinitive instead of a full clause with a main verb:
  'What shall I do next?' she asked. She asked what **to do** next.

- Notice that indirect questions end with a full stop, not a question mark.

D **Put in suitable forms for indirect questions:**

1. 'Do you feel OK?' asked Jean.

   Jean asked _____if_____ I _____felt_____ OK.

2. 'What are you thinking?' I asked.

   I asked her what _____ thinking.

3. 'How were you feeling yesterday?' asked the doctor.

   The doctor asked him how _____

   feeling _____ .

4. 'Has the horse been fed this morning?' asked the vet.

   The vet asked _____ the horse

   _____ been fed _____
   morning.

5. 'Will you be finished by tomorrow?' she asked the painter.

   She asked the painter _____ finished

   by _____ .

6. 'Has everyone gone home?' I wondered.

    I wondered _____ everyone

    _____ gone home.

7. 'Do you want to watch television with us?' they asked the little girl.

    They asked the little girl _____ to

    watch television with _____ .

8. 'How do I switch on the computer?' asked Tom.

    Tom asked how _____ switch on the computer.

9. 'Where shall I put your books?' Mary asked Fred.

    Mary asked Fred where _____ put

    _____ books.

10. 'What do your children call your father's new wife?' she asked him.

    She asked him what _____ children

    _____ father's new wife.

Indirect Commands

- Direct commands use the base form of the verb: **Stop** that noise!
- You use verbs such as **order**, **tell**, **command**, **ask**, **warn**, **advise**, **instruct**, **persuade** to report orders, commands, requests, invitations, advice, instructions, and persuasion. These verbs are followed by an object + **to**-infinitive:

  Mum said to me, 'Close the door quietly.' Mum **told me to close** the door quietly.

  She said to us, 'Don't make a noise.' She **asked us not to make** a noise.

E Complete these indirect commands and requests:

1. 'Sit beside me,' said Harry to Sue.

    Harry invited Sue ___to sit beside him___ .

2. 'Please don't leave me!' Sally said to her brother.

   Sally begged her brother _____ *not to leave her* _____ .

3. 'Company, halt!' shouted the colonel.

   The colonel commanded his company _____ .

4. 'Take a week's holiday,' the doctor said to Dad.

   The doctor advised Dad _____ .

5. The notice says 'Do not enter'.

   The notice forbids us _____ .

6. 'Help me with the beds,' said Mum to me.

   Mum asked me _____ .

7. 'Take care on the steps,' said the guide to the tourists.

   The guide warned the tourists _____ .

8. 'Do stay till tomorrow,' we said to Granny.

   We persuaded Granny _____ .

9. 'Don't look at the answers,' Miss Lee said to us.

   Miss Lee told us _____ .

10. The sign read: 'Please wipe your feet.'

    The sign requested us _____ .

40 PUNCTUATION

- A sentence that makes a statement should end with a full stop.
- A sentence that asks a question should end with a question mark.
- Sentences that express strong feeling should end with an exclamation mark. Greetings can also end with an exclamation mark.
- Although a direct question should end with a question mark, an indirect question should end with a full stop.

A **Put the correct punctuation mark at the end of the following sentences:**

1. Tom had an extra helping of ice-cream

2. Is there anything I can do to help

3. What are you going to do with that

4. What you did was a complete waste of time

5. There's enough for everyone, isn't there

6. Help I'm drowning

7. She asked him what he was intending to do

8. Good morning How are you today

9. You idiot You've broken my favourite vase

10. What I want to know is whether or not you're willing to help us

11. Do you think you could move over a bit

12. Stop that at once

B **Insert commas where they are missing in the following sentences:**

1. Could I have another glass of water please?

2. Excuse me madam. Is that your purse on the floor?

3. Please John don't do that.

4. Oh I'm so glad you managed to come my dear.

5. Come along children. Yes you too James.

6. No no no not these ones! I want those pink ones over there.

7. I'm feeling very well thank you.

8. Yes that's the right answer. Well done lad.

9. Well here you are at last! You know Liz you really ought to try to be more punctual.

10. Believe me it's no fun sleeping in a bus shelter in a thunderstorm.

> ### Commas
>
> ■ A comma is used to separate off from the rest of the sentence words like **please, thank you, yes, no, oh, well**, comments such as **you know** or **that is** or **for example**, and the names of people being spoken to.

More about Commas

- ■ You put a comma between nouns, adjectives and other parts of speech when they come in a list: He was a **tall, thin, bald** man.

- ■ You don't need a comma between adjectives of quite different kinds, for example, size, colour, material (a **little red leather** purse) or quality, origin, type (**complex Japanese electronic** devices). Look at unit 7D again.

- ■ You don't need a comma when there are only two words and they are linked by **and**: He was **tall and thin.**

- ■ In a longer list, if the last two items in the list are linked by **and**, you don't need a comma, though it is not wrong to put one in this position: He was **tall, thin and bald** (or: He was **tall, thin, and bald**).

C **Insert commas where they are missing in the following sentences:**

1. He was followed into the room by a dirty long-haired nasty-looking dog.

2. This is a sure cure for coughs colds chills fevers and all sorts of aches and pains.

3. On the shelf were an odd assortment of boxes bottles and tins.

4. The official languages of Singapore are English Malay Mandarin and Tamil.

5. With eating drinking talking singing and dancing the evening passed all too quickly.

6. He was wearing a brown and grey jacket grey trousers and green boots.

7. I heard a loud eerie almost despairing cry.

8. She spoke rapidly excitedly with eyes flashing.

9. Let's eat drink and be merry.

10. Peter John and I are going to the football match tomorrow.

Apostrophes

- An apostrophe is used to indicate that one or more letters have been left out of a word: **I've** = I have; **doesn't** = does not.

- An apostrophe is used to show who something belongs to: **John's** dog; **John and Peter's** dog; the **boy's** dog (= the dog belonging to the boy); the **boys'** dog (= the dog belonging to the boys); the **children's** dog.

- Remember that **it's** means 'it is' or 'it has', but **its** means 'of it'.

D Put in apostrophes where they are missing in the following sentences:

1. Ill be back in a moment. Dont go away. Weve some things to discuss about next weeks concert.

2. She doesnt know what shes supposed to do.

3. Theyve spent a lot of money on their childrens Christmas presents.

4. Its a lovely little dog, isnt it?

5. Im so glad youve come.

6. Its no wonder that the dogs scratching its ears. Its got fleas.

7. Lets go inside. Ill put on the kettle and well have a nice cup of tea.

8. The teachers searched through every students locker.

9. The teachers searched through both boys lockers.

10. Could you tell me where the mens department is, please?

11. I suppose thats some peoples idea of fun, but it certainly isnt mine.

12. Theres at least three weeks more work to do here.